MW00437968

What if is not?

the

Joy
of INTERCESSION
STUDY GUIDE

DESTINY IMAGE BOOKS BY BENI JOHNSON

Beautiful One

The Happy Intercessor

The Joy of Intercession

Prayer Changes Things

Experiencing the Heavenly Realm with Judy Franklin

Spiritual Java with Bill Johnson

Walking in the Supernatural with Bill Johnson

What if…with Sheri Silk

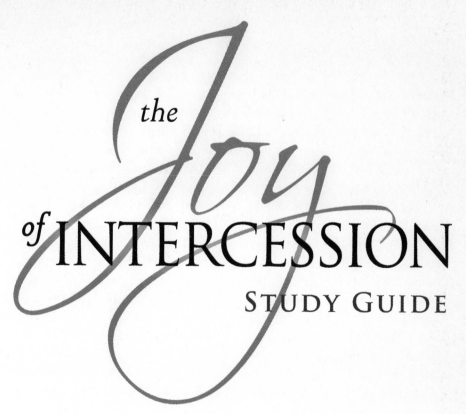

the *Joy* of INTERCESSION

STUDY GUIDE

Becoming a Happy Intercessor

BENI JOHNSON

© Copyright 2013—Beni Johnson

All rights reserved. This book is protected by the copyright laws of the United States of America. This book may not be copied or reprinted for commercial gain or profit. The use of short quotations or occasional page copying for personal or group study is permitted and encouraged. Permission will be granted upon request. Unless otherwise identified, Scripture quotations are taken from the New King James Version. Copyright © 1982 by Thomas Nelson, Inc. Used by permission. All rights reserved. Scripture quotations marked NASB are taken from the NEW AMERICAN STANDARD BIBLE®, Copyright © 1960,1962,1963,1968,1971,1972,1973, 1975,1977,1995 by The Lockman Foundation. Used by permission. Scripture quotations marked AMP are taken from the Amplified® Bible, Copyright © 1954, 1958, 1962, 1964, 1965, 1987 by The Lockman Foundation. Used by permission. Scripture quotations marked MSG are taken from *The Message*. Copyright © 1993, 1994, 1995, 1996, 2000, 2001, 2002. Used by permission of NavPress Publishing Group. Scripture quotations marked KJV are taken from the King James Version. All emphasis within Scripture quotations is the author's own. Please note that Destiny Image's publishing style capitalizes certain pronouns in Scripture that refer to the Father, Son, and Holy Spirit, and may differ from some publishers' styles. Take note that the name satan and related names are not capitalized. We choose not to acknowledge him, even to the point of violating grammatical rules.

DESTINY IMAGE® PUBLISHERS, INC.

P.O. Box 310, Shippensburg, PA 17257-0310

"Promoting Inspired Lives."

This book and all other Destiny Image, Revival Press, MercyPlace, Fresh Bread, Destiny Image Fiction, and Treasure House books are available at Christian bookstores and distributors worldwide.

For a U.S. bookstore nearest you, call 1-800-722-6774.

For more information on foreign distributors, call 717-532-3040.

Reach us on the Internet: www.destinyimage.com.

ISBN 13 TP: 978-0-7684-0341-1

ISBN 13 Ebook: 978-0-7684-8496-0

For Worldwide Distribution, Printed in the U.S.A.

1 2 3 4 5 6 7 8 / 17 16 15 14 13

CONTENTS

INTRODUCTION

$\mathscr{I}$ am so glad that you are taking this six-week journey with me. God is truly changing the way the Body of Christ approaches prayer and intercession. What I bring to this curriculum is nothing more or less than my personal journey. It is my joy to share this with you.

For years, I carried the weight of the world...*and then some*...on my shoulders in the place of intercession. In my book *The Happy Intercessor*, I share my story in much greater detail. I was not always an intercessor. I certainly was not always a *happy* one. However, I will never forget the first time those words were spoken over me over twenty-years ago. A dear friend of ours, prophet Dick Joyce, called me forward and prophesied over me, "You are called to intercession. Not for this season but for a season coming."

At that stage in my life, I was not standing in line waiting to sign up for the role of intercessor. I grew up in a church where the intercessors did not look like happy people most of the time. From my small perspective, all intercessors walked around with what looked to me like very heavy burdens. Weighed down. Sad. Tired. Working. Striving. This is what I thought about intercession. I even remember that as I got older, I thought to myself, *I don't want to be an intercessor.* Why? I did not want to live out what had been modeled to me as a youth. If someone had told me that it was possible for intercessors to be happy, I would have laughed out loud in disbelief. It's amazing how the Holy Spirit changed all of that...

To learn more of my personal testimony on intercession, read the first chapter in *The Happy Intercessor* book. Bits and pieces of it are shared in the following pages in this workbook and in the sessions you will watch. However, the full version of my testimony is in the book.

This curriculum is my best attempt to help raise up a new generation of intercessors in this strategic moment of history. This truly is the "season coming" that Dick Joyce prophesied about. God desires a people who pray out of a place of intimacy and joy with Him; and in turn these intercessors declare solutions over the problems that plague our lives, cities, and nations.

My definition for being an intercessor is *capturing the heartbeat of Heaven and declaring or praying that into my world. It's true agreement with Heaven.* This is what we are going to learn in the weeks ahead. More than going over a list of prayer formulas and principles, I believe you are going to experience a deeper level of intimacy with the Father. Out of that joyful place where you grasp His heart, know His ways, and catch His vision, you will begin releasing His world into your world through the joyful place of intercession.

Blessings,

Beni Johnson
Pastor, Bethel Redding

USING THIS STUDY GUIDE

As a participant in this curriculum, here is how you will be using this study guide in the weeks ahead:

Small Group/Class Sessions

Whether you are going through these six lessons in a small group, class, or individually, you will be watching the videos and filling in some blanks as you go through the actual sessions (an answer key is in the back of the workbook). We keep the fill-in-the-blanks to a minimum, as we want you to write down the insights that stand out specifically to you and give you the freedom to record what the Holy Spirit shares with you during the sessions.

Daily Devotional Reading

There are five daily devotional readings per week. These are designed to reinforce the material you studied and discussed during your actual session. In all, both the readings and answering the reflection questions should not take you more than 15-20 minutes per day.

Daily Reflection Questions

These questions help personalize the material you have been studying, giving you the opportunity for Bible study and personal reflection.

Daily Meditation

This statement captures the essence of the day's focus.

Prayer

This prayer is totally customizable. In fact, it is designed to be a launching pad for you to enter into your own personal time of prayer and intercession with the Lord. More than just studying concepts, principles, and formulas, this curriculum is truly interactive. The goal is not for you to receive a bunch of good information, rather the purpose of it is for you to actually *discuss what you are learning with the Holy Spirit,* and ask the Lord for wisdom, revelation, and direction on how to incorporate these tools into your prayer life.

For Additional Study

These resources are *not* mandatory for this study, but are strongly recommended. *The Happy Intercessor* book provides the foundational material for what is presented in the video sessions; however, most of the material in this study guide is all new and simply based on the subject matter presented in the book. To maximize this study, we recommend that you purchase a copy of *The Happy Intercessor* and *The Joy of Intercession* devotional.

DISCOVERING HOW TO PRAY FROM GOD'S HEART

"When I pray from the heart of God, I become so lost in the presence of God that it feels like the only thing I am listening to is the voice of God. In that place, His heart, His plans, His voice become so real it is almost like we become one. At those times, it feels like I pray *with* Him. When I am in that place, all I have to do is agree with God and partner with the things that are already on His heart. Those are the times when we pray together, and I begin to co-labor with God through my prayers. Those are the times when I begin to see real breakthrough."

—BENI JOHNSON

Session 1

Discovering How to Pray from God's Heart

Discussion Questions

Keys to Praying from God's Heart:

Key 1: Your intercession is birthed through _____ with the Lord.

Key 2: Your intimacy with God, through intercession, exposes you to the _____ and _____ of God for the world.

Key 3: Let go of your _____ when you come before the Lord in the secret place.

Key 4: Be _____ to the move of the Holy Spirit during intercession.

Key 5: Believe that God actually likes your _____.

Day One

CAPTURING THE HEARTBEAT OF HEAVEN

Your kingdom come. Your will be done, on earth as it is in heaven (Matthew 6:10).

Our culture at Bethel Church is committed to seeing God's world invade this one. *The Lord's Prayer* offers some of the clearest evidence that Father God desires to see the climate and atmosphere that defines Heaven birthed here on earth.

There are many ways we have experienced "Heaven invading earth" over the years. We have seen signs, wonders, healings, and miracles that continually fill us with awe and wonder for our great God. We have experienced unusual manifestations of God's glory that both leave us speechless and send our children running into His Presence, wide-eyed and ready to embrace their Father.

To see Heaven released into the earth, we first need to grasp what Heaven looks like. I call this capturing the heartbeat of Heaven. This is where prayer and intercession begins. It begins with Him and His world. You see, everything in Heaven is a reflection of the glorious Center of Heaven—the Father. For us to truly know what Heaven is like, it is important that we know what He is like. This is truly the joy of intercession. In this place, we get to know and experience our God in the most unique and wonderful ways.

One of the most important things that happens is that as we get to know Him, we get to know what's in His mind and on His heart. These are the things He wants to do. These are the things special to Him, and He lets you and me in on these plans through intercession.

EVERYTHING IN HEAVEN IS A REFLECTION OF THE GLORIOUS CENTERPIECE OF HEAVEN—THE FATHER.

In the weeks ahead, we are going to focus on this joyful place of intercession and how being an intercessor enables you and me to capture the heartbeat of Heaven. Since our mission is to represent (or *re*-present) Jesus to the world, it is so important that we do it accurately. All of us could agree that there have been many images and examples of a "Jesus" that have been displayed over the years that are not in line with His character and nature. Why is this? Many have pursued principles and formulas above intimacy, and as a result, the image they project tends to be lacking in love, compassion, and character.

When our delight is knowing and capturing the Father's heart, the image of Him and His world that we show to this world will increase in accuracy. It will increase in power. It will increase in breakthrough. Get ready to experience an increase of His world breaking into this one as we journey to the joyful place of intercession!

Daily Reflection Questions

1. Read Matthew 6:10. Based on this Scripture, what does it mean for God's world to invade this one?

---

2. Why is knowing God's heart so important when it comes to representing Him to the world?

_____

_____

_____

3. How will learning about intercession help you to capture God's heart in a greater way?

_____

_____

_____

_____

Daily Meditation

Intercession enables us to capture the heartbeat of Heaven and accurately represent Jesus on Earth.

Prayer

> *Father, Your will is to see Your world break into this one. Show me how to be a carrier of Heaven's heartbeat in the days and weeks to come as I learn about intercession. Renew my mind according to Your Word. Transform the way I pray and interact with You so that I experience your heart and character in ways I never have before.*
> *In Jesus' name,*
> *Amen*

For Additional Study

- Read *The Happy Intercessor*, pages 27-28.

- Read *The Joy of Intercession* devotional, pages 21-26.

Matt 6:10 Define Prayer & Intercession
1-5 Benefits of intercession

INTERCESSORS: THE WOMBS OF GOD

*"He who believes in Me, as the Scripture said,
'From his innermost being will flow rivers of
living water'"* (John 7:38 NASB).

*I*n this passage, as Jesus talks about rivers that flow from the *innermost being*, He is using language that describes a "womb." This Scripture would go on to be fulfilled at the outpouring of the Holy Spirit at Pentecost—and is now an available reality to every believer.

Because of the Holy Spirit, you and I are able to be wombs of God, creating and birthing the things of Heaven through our intercession. To continue along these lines, we become pregnant with the purposes of Heaven in that place of intimacy with God. Just as natural intimacy produces conception and life, so does spiritual intimacy in the secret place with the Father bring forth life as well.

In these early sessions and daily exercises, I will talk about intimacy with God a great deal. It is the essential key to joyful intercession.

INTIMACY IS THE ESSENTIAL KEY TO JOYFUL INTERCESSION.

The fruit of our intimacy with God are Heaven-birthed plans, purposes, and desires. God shares His heart with those who long to know

Him, and in that place of intimate exchange, the things that are on God's heart work their way into our hearts. We are co-laborers with God, right? He is sovereign and able to do all things; and yet, He has made a choice to bring His purposes to pass, on earth, through His people—you and me. Through prayer and intercession, we actually learn what His desires are. In turn, we fulfill our role as co-laborers by praying and declaring His desires to come to pass.

How does this all happen? Through intimacy. It is not enough to guess what God wants accomplished in this world—we must *know*. The wonderful truth is, intercession positions you and me to *know* what is on the heart of God, and then become filled with His will. What an incredible thought! We talk about knowing God's will, but in essence, He wants us to know it and *be filled with it*. His vision is for you and me to be the people who actually give birth to His will, His purposes, His plans, and His dreams on the planet.

Daily Reflection Questions

1. Read John 7:37-39. What does it mean to be a womb of God?

_____

_____

_____

_____

2. How are the plans and purposes of God birthed in us?

_____

_____

_____

_____

3.   What has God specifically birthed inside of you during times of in-
     timacy and relationship with Him? (Could be dreams, visions, goals,
     ideas, etc.)

_____

_____

_____

_____

_____

Daily Meditation

As an intercessor, you are a womb through which God has chosen to
birth His will and purposes into the earth.

Prayer

*Thank You, Father, for the blessing of co-laboring with You. It
is an honor that You have chosen to birth Your will and purposes
in my heart and use my life to accomplish them in the earth. I
embrace this call and identity with great joy. Have your way,
Holy Spirit.*
In Jesus' name,
Amen

For Additional Study

- Read *The Happy Intercessor*, pages 30-31.

- Read *The Joy of Intercession* devotional, pages 47-50.

BREAK THE HANDCUFFS

*Whatever God has promised gets stamped with the
Yes of Jesus. In him, this is what we preach and
pray, the great Amen, God's Yes and our Yes together,
gloriously evident* (2 Corinthians 1:20 MSG).

Even though God is limitless, there are ways we can actually experience Him in limited ways. This is obviously not His will for us. This is very common in prayer and intercession, as we enter our time with the Father with a preconceived idea and agenda of what should or should not take place. Sometimes our prayer cards and prayer lists actually restrain us from hearing His voice or experiencing breakthrough. Are these things inherently bad? *Absolutely not.* Time after time, Scripture encourages us to bring our requests and petitions before the Lord.

I am talking less about prayer cards and prayer requests, and more so about how we think God should respond during our times of prayer and intercession. Maybe He wants to engage you in dialogue about that prayer request. Maybe that particular request or prayer list is not what He wants to talk about during this particular time of prayer. There are so many options, namely because God is a multifaceted living Person. When we reduce an experiential relationship with God to formulas and principles, we actually handcuff God and prevent ourselves from experiencing the supernatural partnership He longs to enjoy with us.

LISTEN TO THE HEARTBEAT OF GOD.

When it comes to intercession, we must listen to the heartbeat of God and not always just present our "stuff" to Him. He is interested in our lives, but at the same time, our call as intercessors is to be interested in what interests *Him*. It is easy for us to come before God with our lists and make those items the focus of our time with Him. There is a time and place for this, absolutely. At the same time, we must approach intercession relationally. It is not formulaic. It is an exchange with a relational God who wants to talk. He wants to talk to you, and there is a good chance He also wants to talk *through* you.

There are promises that God wants you to pray into and release that have His guaranteed seal of approval on them, the divine "Yes" of Jesus (see 2 Cor. 1:20). To tap into these promises and participate in their release, it is important that we approach God with ears to hear and a heart open to receive what He wants to share in our times of intercession.

Daily Reflection Questions

1. How can we handcuff God in the way we approach prayer and intercession?

   _____

   _____

   _____

2. Think of some examples in prayer/intercession where you have approached God with open ears and an open heart—agenda free. List three things that He shared with you in those times that produced breakthrough in your life, or someone else's.

   _____

   _____

   _____

   _____

Daily Meditation

✳There is no limit to what God can speak to and release through us when we approach Him with surrendered agendas.

Prayer

You are a Limitless God! Thank You, Father, that I get to hear your heart and release Your promises into my life, and into the world, through intercession. I come to You with no agenda except to hear what's on Your heart. Give me ears to hear what You are saying "Yes" to so I can come into agreement with it and see Your promises come to pass.
In Jesus' name,
Amen

For Additional Study

- Read *The Happy Intercessor*, pages 31-33.

- Read *The Joy of Intercession* devotional, pages 51-54.

GOD LIKES YOUR IDEAS

*But the Lord said to my father David, "Whereas it was
in your heart to build a temple for My name, you did
well that it was in your heart"* (1 Kings 8:18).

God chose David to do incredible things through because he was
a man who would say, "Yes." It does not take long after reading the
Psalms of King David to see that this man enjoyed a deep relationship
with God. It was truly in those moments of intimacy, and in the over-
flow of that intimacy, that ideas and dreams were birthed in his heart.
The same is true for you and me.

When we believe that God actually likes *our* ideas, we are embold-
ened to pray from a place of security. Remember, prayer and intercession
is our part in this wonderful co-laboring relationship that God has set
up. He chose free-thinking, creative people to be integral parts in bringing His Kingdom to the earth. He knew exactly what He was getting
into, and actually delights in the fact that He gets to work with our
creativity and our ideas in the process. We have this security in prayer
because we are confident that *God likes our ideas,* whether He directly
placed the idea in our mind or not!

**IN MOMENTS OF INTIMACY, IDEAS AND
DREAMS ARE BIRTHED IN YOUR HEART.**

There comes a point in the place of intimacy with the Lord, where we become so intertwined with Him, and so in tune with His voice and ideas, that when it comes to who actually came up with an idea—us or God—it's really tough to say. Either it was an idea directly birthed by God, or it was an idea that we came up with that was born out of His influence. Either way, the idea, the dream, the vision carries His heartbeat and His purpose. God's DNA is all over it just because we are created in His image and are operating out of that identity.

Remember, the key to experiencing breakthrough in prayer is the agreement of God's *Yes* and our *yes*. When our ideas are in agreement with His, whether He directly placed the idea in our heart or not, we are working with something that has the potential to release significant breakthrough.

Daily Reflection Questions

1. Read First Kings 8:18 again. Why do you think God liked David's ideas and dreams?

   _____

   _____

   _____

   _____

2. Recall some of your most memorable and transformational times of intimacy with the Lord. Were any ideas, dreams, or visions birthed out of those times of deep relationship? If so, list them below.

   _____

   _____

   _____

   _____

3.   Pause for a moment and reflect: what are some ideas, dreams, and visions that are on your heart *right now*. Don't be quick to dismiss them if they don't immediately sound or feel spiritual. Take this time to: 1) Write them down, and 2) after doing so, review them carefully and look for the character/nature of God in them. They may not have come directly *from* God, but they very well may be ideas that He likes!

Daily Meditation

God likes your ideas. Whether He birthed the idea *directly* in your heart, or you came up with the idea (and it in some way reflects His heart), He likes it!

Daily Prayer

Lord, thank You for the ability to dream and imagine. Show me what it means to understand that You actually like and value my ideas. For the ideas that I have cast aside, put on hold, or even thrown away—Lord, I pray for a resurrection of every single one that says "Yes" to Your plans and purposes for my life and for this world.
In Jesus' name,
Amen

For Additional Study

- Read *The Happy Intercessor*, pages 33-35.

- Read *The Joy of Intercession* devotional, pages 55-57.

FOCUSED ON HIS VOICE

*The voice of the Lord is powerful; the voice of
the Lord is full of majesty* (Psalm 29:4).

When you are locked into the voice of the Lord, it is amazing how
everything else fades into the background. Let me illustrate.

I remember when my daughter, Leah, was having her first child.
She asked me to coach her through the pregnancy. I had delivered my
three children naturally, and she wanted to follow suit. Such an honor.
I so clearly recall that experience, particularly the climate of the labor
room. You see, in a natural birth, you can invite friends and family into
the labor room with you.

Leah is very social and enjoyed having friends and family visiting up
until the time of the birth. Toward the end of the labor comes the most
intense time. This demands all of your concentration just to make it
through the contractions. This is where we were. Moments would come
when I would release peace over Leah, and then the focus was all on her
part to listen to my instructions.

Well, at one of these intense moments, one of our friends came into
the room and began talking—not necessarily paying attention to the
intensity of what was going on. I was amazed that Leah seemed to be
OK with it all. After the delivery, I asked her about the distraction in the
room. What she told me released a powerful revelation of intercession.

Leah said that she didn't really notice the distraction because she was so focused on *my voice* and what I was telling her to do.

> IN THE MIDST OF DISTRACTION, PARTNER
> WITH GOD, LISTEN TO HIS VOICE, AND
> PRAY HIS HEART INTO BEING.

When God gives us strategies to pray—you know, the ones that we burn with—we can become so focused on His thundering voice that we don't become distracted. Life is like that labor room. There are endless opportunities for distraction as we simply walk through the everyday human experience. While we must engage with what is going on around us, we can be like my daughter. In the midst of distraction, we continue to partner with God, listen to His voice, and pray His heart into being. For us, His voice thunders above everything else (see Ps. 29:3).

This is what God is looking to raise up in His intercessors. A people who are able to go through life, not separated and detached from everything, but *at the same time,* so locked into His voice, so fixed on His gaze, so pressed into His heart, that they are able to bring His purposes to pass in this world, through prayer, as they walk through everyday life!

Daily Reflection Questions

1. Read Psalm 29:3-9. Using these verses, describe the voice of the Lord and what each description means to you.

    ▪ _____

    ▪ _____

    ▪ _____

    ▪ _____

2. How does staying focused on the voice of the Lord drown out all of the distractions and noise in the world?

_____

_____

_____

3. Think of a time in your life when you had the opportunity to be distracted (by problems, circumstances, situations, etc.), *but* continued to focus on the voice of the Lord. Why is it important to stay focused on God's voice and what He is saying, regardless of what's going on around us?

_____

_____

_____

Daily Meditation

As we keep focused on God's voice—no matter what is going on around us—we remain in a place where we are able to birth His plans and purposes into the earth through prayer.

Daily Prayer

> *Your voice is my focus. No matter what is going on around me, I chose to keep my ears in tune with what You're saying. Distractions, circumstances, and busyness will not rob me from hearing your heart and releasing Your purposes through prayer.*
> *In Jesus' name,*
> *Amen*

For Additional Study

- Read *The Happy Intercessor*, pages 35-37.

- Read *The Joy of Intercession* devotional, page 58.

KEYS TO PRAYING FROM THE PLACE OF VICTORY

"As intercessors, our job is to call the plays. We are the offensive team. If we don't understand that we are praying from a place of victory, we will be intercessors whose prayer lives are marked with defeat. This is how intercessors live an offensive lifestyle—they pray according to God's plans, and they pray from a place of victory."

—BENI JOHNSON

Session 2

Keys to Praying from the Place of Victory

Discussion Questions

Principles to Praying from the Place of Victory:

Victory Principle 1: Intercession should always be on the _____.

Victory Principle 2: Do not _____.

Victory Principle 3: Focus on God's _____ plan in every situation.

Victory Principle 4: Keep your prayers _____ and hitting the _____.

Victory Principle 5: Find God's heart and will in God's _____.

Victory Principle 6: Do not call down _____ and powers.

Victory Principle 7: There is no prayer that is _____ to God.

Day One

INTERCESSION ON
THE OFFENSE

*As a result, we are no longer to be children, tossed
here and there by waves and carried about by every
wind of doctrine, by the trickery of men, by craftiness
in deceitful scheming* (Ephesians 4:14 NASB).

In the game of football, you have a defensive team and an offensive team. The defensive team is always trying to steal the football away from the opposing offensive team. The offensive team, on the other hand, calls the plays since they have the ball. They have the advantage and the upper hand on the field.

We need to understand that, as intercessors, we stand in this upper-hand advantage spiritually. Somewhere along the line, prayer became reactionary and defensive in purpose. This should not be so. For too long, we have been begging for what already belongs to us or running around after the enemy. It has all been in the defensive posture. It is time to see that God has armed us with intercession so that we can pray out of a place of victory, for the people of God are the very people who should carry the ball and call the shots in the spirit realm.

It is essential that we get this settled up front; for if you do not understand that you pray from a place of victory, you will be an intercessor whose prayer life is marked with defeat. You will constantly be fighting and wrestling, not only with the enemy, but also with God. You will be contending, pleading, and crying out for things He has already purchased for you on Calvary. The key is praying *from* victory, not *for* victory. We don't pray *for* victory because it has already been won. So much of what we call prayer has become just that. We are fighting for what we already have, and this keeps us from claiming new ground for the Kingdom. Calvary must settle the issue for us.

CALVARY HAS SETTLED EVERY ISSUE.

Like an offensive team on the football field, we need to have confidence that God has designed and destined us to win. As those who pray and intercede from an offensive position, our job is to take the land and not waste our time running around after the enemy, trying to steal the ball from him. We need to remember that he lost the ball, and he lost authority at Calvary.

The enemy would love us to be like the people Paul described in Ephesians 4:14, *tossed here and there* and *carried around*. No stability. No footing. That cannot be us. Those on the offense are focused. Their eyes are fixed on victory. They are confident because they call the shots, they execute the plays, and they carry the ball. This is who we are in the spirit. We pray according to God's plans and pray from a place of ultimate victory.

Daily Reflection Questions

1.   What does it mean to pray from the place of victory?

_____

_____

_____

_____

_____

2. Why is it important to pray from an "offensive" posture rather than a defensive one?

_____

_____

_____

3. What are some areas in your life where you need to pray from a place of victory?

_____

_____

_____

Daily Meditation

We don't pray *for* victory; we pray *from* a place of victory. It has already been won!

Prayer

I praise You, Lord, because my victory was purchased at the Cross. I do not need to pray for it, but You have enabled me to pray from this place of victory. Because of Calvary, I am on the offense. Father, show me what it means to live a lifestyle where I call the shots in the spirit realm and release Your Kingdom.
In Jesus' name,
Amen

For Additional Study

- Read *The Happy Intercessor*, pages 39-41.

- Read *The Joy of Intercession* devotional, pages 59-62.

Day Two

INTERCESSION THAT HITS THE MARK

*...and my message and my preaching were not in
persuasive words of wisdom, but in demonstration of
the Spirit and of power...* (1 Corinthians 2:4).

Apostle Paul was a man intent on hitting the mark. He lived an offensive lifestyle and operated from a place of victory, just as we have been studying. His success, however, was not attributed to human reason, although Paul is renowned for being a highly educated and learned man. We see in First Corinthians 2:4-5 that his ministry was not effective because of some natural means—it was infused with the power of God. He leaned on Another Source and experienced supernatural success. He hit the mark because He laid aside his ideas and strategies about how things should work, and rather came into alignment with the Lord's plan.

This is vital for us to understand as we continue our journey into intercession. Effective intercessors know how to listen for the plays that God calls, and they know how to catch the ball and make the touchdown (continuing with our football analogy). In fact, one of the meanings for the word intercession is to "strike the mark." The key to striking the mark is modeling Apostle Paul and coming into alignment with the thoughts and purposes of the Lord.

TO CAPTURE GOD'S HEART AND PRAY EFFECTIVELY, PRAY WHAT IS WRITTEN IN SCRIPTURE.

How do we become targeted in our prayers and actually know God's heart? After all, concepts start to sound abstract when there is no definition given to them. I never want our pursuit of God's heart to be some abstract idea. It all begins with the Bible. In fact, the Torah means "to shoot straight" or "hit the mark." If we want to capture God's heart and pray effectively, we start by praying what is written in Scripture.

Praying the Word is a great way to pray the heart of God. It's all right there in writing. However, the written word is waiting for your prayer and proclamation! The Kingdom is released through our decrees.

I recommend taking a chapter or small section of Scripture and starting to think or meditate upon that particular Scripture. Read the verses over and over, slowly. As you do, they will begin to sink into your spirit. They become alive in your heart and in your mind. Before long, you will find yourself praying from those verses. You will never cease to hit the mark when your prayers are bathed in God's Word. After all, you are saying what He is saying, and His Word *always* produces!

Daily Reflection Questions

1. What made Apostle Paul's ministry and preaching effective, according to First Corinthians 2:4?

_____

_____

_____

2. How does Scripture help us "hit the mark" in our prayers?

_____

_____

_____

3.   Find a passage of Scripture. Perhaps start with the Psalms. Read it. Review it. Meditate upon it. Then start to pray that Scripture. What did the Lord say or do through this time of praying the Scriptures?

_____

_____

_____

_____

Daily Meditation

To hit the mark in intercession and experience results, we need to follow God's plan rather than human reasoning. Often this involves praying the Scriptures.

Prayer

> *Holy Spirit, as I pray, show me how to hit the mark. Open my eyes to Your wonderful Word. Reveal Scriptures to me that I should start praying and declaring, to see Your will accomplished. As I say what You are saying, I will experience what You have promised.*
> *In Jesus' name,*
> *Amen*

For Additional Study

- Read *The Happy Intercessor*, pages 43-47.

- Read *The Joy of Intercession* devotional, pages 67-70.

Day Three

INTERCESSION THAT ENFORCES A PERSPECTIVE OF VICTORY

And do not be conformed to this world, but be transformed by the renewing of your mind... (Romans 12:2).

*T*hough we intercede from a place of victory, the reality is that there are also mindsets and strongholds that need to be addressed. For example, one of the targets that we have in our prayers at Bethel is that we believe God has promised us a cancer-free zone. This is one of our number one prayers. We are focused and determined to "hit the mark" on this one and see that evil disease destroyed in an entire region.

We have experienced tremendous victory in this area, as we have seen so many healed of cancer. At the same time, we have seen people die with this disease. The key is perseverance. We are confident that as we continue to carry prayer down the field, we know that we will hit the mark and reach the goal. We're not fighting to get something, but rather, we are fighting to enforce something. Let me explain.

How we "fight" demands a change of thinking and perspective. Our minds need to be renewed on this subject. There is no need for us to convince God that a cancer-free zone is a good idea. We don't need to beg, plead, and "fight" in the place of intercession to get God on the same page as we are. In this particular arena, cancer has already been defeated at Calvary. If we want God's opinion on disease, we should look no further than the Cross. We are not fighting to defeat cancer; it has already been dealt with. We are fighting to enforce the work of Calvary over that disease, in our region.

THE BIBLE IS YOUR ROADMAP TO GOD'S HEART.

Even though the differences seem small, I assure you, they are not. There are so many out there who do not believe God's will is to heal disease; and rather than enforcing the finished work of the Cross over their bodies or over their regions to see disease defeated, they are wrestling with God, trying to convince Him that healing is a good idea to start with. This type of fight is wasted energy, and God does not want us spending our time and energy in intercession trying to convince Him that certain things are good ideas.

As we studied yesterday, the Bible is our roadmap to God's heart. It reveals who He is and what His will is. Jesus is the ultimate expression of the Father and His will. How did Jesus handle disease? Healing. How did Jesus handle torment? He brought freedom. How did Jesus deal with storms? He calmed them. The Scriptures and the model of Jesus are everything we need when going into the place of intercession and securing a victorious perspective.

Daily Reflection Questions

1. What is the difference between fighting to convince God to do something and fighting to enforce God's will?

_____

_____

_____

2. Why do we need our minds renewed when it comes to understanding the fight we are engaged in?

_____

_____

_____

3. List some areas in your life where you are persevering to enforce God's will in prayer?

_____

_____

_____

Daily Meditation

Jesus has already secured our victory; the fight in intercession has everything to do with enforcing what Jesus already purchased, releasing it *on earth as it is in Heaven.*

Prayer

> *Holy Spirit, renew my mind according to Your Word and Your truth. I am not asking for victory. Jesus paid it all so I could be victorious. Rather, I am enforcing Jesus' victory on earth. Show me areas where I can enforce His victory through prayer and intercession. Show me areas in my life, in my family, in my city, in my region—in any area of life You choose to reveal to me— that needs what my intercession brings to the table in enforcing the victory of the Cross.*
> *In Jesus' name,*
> *Amen*

For Additional Study

- Read *The Happy Intercessor*, pages 47-48.

- Read *The Joy of Intercession* devotional, pages 75-78.

INTERCESSION THAT IS GOD-FOCUSED, NOT CRISIS-FOCUSED

Of the sons of Issachar, men who understood the times, with knowledge of what Israel should do, their chiefs were two hundred; and all their kinsmen were at their command (1 Chronicles 12:32 NASB).

The sons of Issachar give us an excellent example of prophetic intercession. This term, "prophetic intercession" means different things to different people, but ultimately, it has everything to do with discerning and understanding the times—and responding in agreement with God's heart.

God gives prophetic insight or discernment on a matter for a purpose. For example, if someone is given prophetic information about an on-coming crisis, it is never for the purpose of simply declaring the crisis. If a hurricane, tornado, or some other type of natural disaster is coming, and we are given supernatural insight into its coming, our job is to follow the example of the sons of Issachar. They were not just discerners. They did not simply understand the times and talk about how evil they were. On the contrary, their focus was on what *Israel should do*, the key word being "do."

They had a plan. Not only were they given unusual insight and prophetic discernment about the times in which they were living, but they knew what to do about it. Again, we must follow their example if we are going to truly birth God's Kingdom, on earth, through our intercession.

Ensure your focus is God and His solution rather than the crisis.

God's purposes are not birthed when we focus on the crisis. Whether we receive insight about some type of crisis through prophetic revelation or simply acknowledge the hostile climate around us, solutions will never be brought to the table as long as we focus on the problems. However, when He is our focus, His will, His ways, and His strategies will become the very thing we release, through intercession, into crisis.

As prayer pastor at Bethel Church, I get a lot of emails from all around the world. Many of them are asking for emergency prayer or have designated their prayer request as a "high alert." I will read some of them. Many are good, but many of them are so full of fear that I cannot entertain them. Before I engage the prayer request, I must ensure my focus is God and His solution rather than being consumed with the crisis.

We need to carry the same perspective with us into the place of intercession. It is easy to become consumed by the crisis. However, that produces no fruit except fear. We need to keep our focus fixed on God and respond to the crisis with His solutions if we are going to witness the breakthrough He desires.

Daily Reflection Questions

1. What was unique about the sons of Issachar, according to First Chronicles 12:32?

_____

_____

_____

_____

2. How can we follow their model in our approach to intercession?

_____

_____

_____

3. List some specific prayer requests (either personal or for other people in your life), and beside them write God's solutions to those problems.

PRAYER REQUEST	GOD'S SOLUTION

Daily Meditation

In intercession, we must be God-focused, not crisis-focused, if we are going to release breakthrough and solutions.

Prayer

Father, help me be like the sons of Issachar. May I respond to crises, problems, and circumstances by releasing Your solutions through intercession. I refuse to become consumed by the crisis and fear; instead, I keep my eyes on You. Your greatness. Your faithfulness. Your power. Your glory. May Your Word and Your Kingdom be released as I declare Your solutions over crises.
In Jesus' name,
Amen

For Additional Study

- Read *The Happy Intercessor*, pages 48-49.

INTERCESSION THAT RELEASES MULTIPLIED POWER

"...perhaps the Lord will work for us, for the Lord is not restrained to save by many or by few" (1 Samuel 14:6 NASB).

God is looking for intercessors who are passionate for Him and His Kingdom to come. They are unafraid of releasing God's promises and solutions into the earth, enforcing His victory into every realm that demands it, even if it is just one person, or a small company of intercessors being the ones carrying this mandate. Let me give you an illustration from the Old Testament.

In First Samuel 14, we read about Jonathan—King Saul's son—who represents the stance we as intercessors should take. At this time, King Saul was sitting under a pomegranate tree, obviously more interested in his comfort than confronting Israel's enemy, the Philistines. Israel was desperate for their king to fight. Jonathan, on the other hand, was fed up with nothing being done and took a powerful stance. He secretly took his armor bearer and went out to take on the whole Philistine camp. Two men against the entire army of the Philistines!

Jonathan's attitude represents how we should engage intercession. Remember, we already have the victory. The fight is fixed and Calvary bought it all. Whether you have an army of ten thousand people standing with you, or if it is just you and a like-faithed friend, numbers mean little when it comes to the power in intercession. Remember how God whittled down Gideon's army? Effective intercession has nothing to do with our natural strength and ability, and everything to do with the One whose supernatural power is released when we begin interceding.

Your intercession carries the potential to win battles, release destiny, and transform the impossible.

When we recognize that the power and presence of God is released because of intercession, our confidence receives a significant boost. The same was true for Jonathan. His confidence was nothing short of supernatural. Why? Reread First Samuel 14:6. The key phrase that reveals his heart and exposes the source of his confidence is—"*for the Lord is not restrained to save by many or by few.*" The New Living Translation phrases it this way: *He [God] can win a battle whether He has many warriors or only a few!*

The common denominator for Jonathan was God. The same is true for us. You carry a multitude of power in your intercession. In the same manner that Jonathan recognized the multiplied power that accompanied him, we must likewise know that our intercession carries the potential to win battles, release destiny, and transform the impossible.

Daily Reflection Questions

1. Read First Samuel 14:1-15. What are some attitudes and postures that you can apply to intercession from Jonathan's brave example?

_____

_____

_____

2. How does intercession release multiplied power?

_____

_____

_____

3. Recall specific things you have interceded for in the past. Write down three instances where you interceded for something that demanded a miracle—and it happened!

    a. _____

    _____

    b. _____

    _____

    c. _____

    _____

This exercise is designed for *you* to get you in the habit of keeping record of the miraculous things God has done—specifically because of your intercession. Remembering testimonies builds your faith and strengthens your confidence in the multiplied power that intercession releases.

Daily Meditation

Your intercession carries and releases multiplied power.

Prayer

Lord, just like Jonathan, I stand confident—not in my own strength or ability—but in Your power that's released through intercession. Thank You, Lord, for this mighty Kingdom tool. As I open my mouth and declare the things on Your heart, I believe Your presence is released. Your power invades that situation and Your will is accomplished. I don't need an army; I simply need You, and trust that Your power is sufficient.
In Jesus' name,
Amen

For Additional Study

- Read *The Happy Intercessor*, pages 55-59.

SECRETS TO PRAYING LIKE JESUS

"Jesus had experienced great joy in Heaven. All of Heaven is joy. The Bible says we will enter into the joy of the Lord one day. While Jesus lived on this earth, I believe that He knew how to live out of this supernatural joy, even in suffering. Remember, Jesus is our perfect example of how to live here on earth. We believe as a people of God's power that we are to bring Heaven to earth. Jesus revealed that joy is a very big part of Heaven. Heaven is filled with joy. It is our responsibility to bring that here on earth through intercession."

—BENI JOHNSON

Session 3

Secrets to Praying Like Jesus

Discussion Questions

To pray like Jesus...

We model _____.

We cannot carry _____ or _____.

We must get God's _____.

We use the same _____
that He did.

Day One

THE JOY OF KNOWING GOD'S PLAN...AND PARTICIPATING IN IT!

looking unto Jesus, the author and finisher of our faith,
who for the joy that was set before Him endured the
cross, despising the shame, and has sat down at the
right hand of the throne of God (Hebrews 12:2).

*I*ntercessors ought to be the happiest people on the planet. Why? Because they know the plans of God *and* get to participate in seeing them released into the earth. This is why Jesus was so full of joy, even in embracing the Cross.

Hebrews 12:2 describes what Jesus was willing to endure because of the *joy set before Him.* As dark of a day that Calvary was, and as difficult as it was for Jesus to experience, Scripture tells us that He possessed a motivating vision of joy. He was tapped into the plans of God, and was participating in seeing them released. What an example for us as intercessors to follow!

Jesus was confronted with crisis after crisis. The crisis of the Cross. The crisis of everything that led up to the Cross. The crisis of sin. The crisis of death. The crisis of betrayal. And yet Jesus is not defined by any of these crisis events. Jesus endured them and ultimately overcame them. They were all a means to an end. The end was salvation. The end was a reality where God lived inside of humanity. The end was transformed cities and discipled nations. In short, Jesus was a man of joy because His eyes were fixed on the joyous purpose and plan of the Father. Not only that, but as our Mediator, He was the key participant in bringing God's purpose to pass. We must follow Jesus' example, as intercessors serve as mediators between Heaven and earth.

You are in relationship with and connected to the same Source as Jesus—the Father.

Intercession deals with crisis. Not all of the time, though. It would be incorrect for us to define intercession as reactionary only. In other words, we cannot treat intercession as something we only do when a crisis is happening and we need to bring Heaven's solution into the situation. As we have studied so far, intercession involves intimately capturing the heartbeat of Heaven. Even in dealing with crisis, we do it from a position of intimacy. We respond to situations the same way Jesus would because we are in relationship with and connected to the same Source that Jesus was—the Father.

We begin to model Jesus as intercessors when we follow His example as One who, through intimacy, knew the plans of the Father, and through His obedience brought these plans to pass in the earth.

Daily Reflection Questions

1. Read Hebrews 12:2. What do you think caused Jesus to endure suffering with joy?

_____

_____

_____

_____

_____

2. Even though Jesus experienced crisis, He did not focus on it. Instead, He was focused on the plan of the Father coming to pass through His obedience. How does Jesus' example provide a model for intercession?

_____

_____

_____

_____

3. In what ways have you endured something because you were motivated by the positive end result?

_____

_____

_____

_____

Daily Meditation

Jesus was full of joy—even when going to the Cross—because He knew God's plan and got to participate in bringing it to pass. As intercessors, we get to do the same thing.

Prayer

Father, may my focus be Your plans and Your purposes. I know there is crisis in the world. I know there are circumstances and suffering. I also know that Jesus endured suffering because of the joy He experienced from knowing Your good plan and bringing it to pass. As an intercessor, I thank You for the ability to know Your good plan and participate in seeing it released on earth.
In Jesus' name,
Amen

For Additional Study

- Read *The Happy Intercessor*, pages 76-77.

- Read *The Joy of Intercession* devotional, pages 91-94.

THE JOY OF JESUS' FINISHED WORK

Therefore when Jesus had received the sour wine,
He said, "It is finished!" And He bowed His head
and gave up His spirit (John 19:30 NASB).

The ultimate foundation for us as intercessors is the finished work of Jesus. We have already talked about what it means to fight *from* victory instead of fighting *for* it. In order to truly understand this principle, we must look at the example of Jesus.

It is very important that as intercessors we have a revelation of what Jesus did while He was here on the earth. Jesus came to set the captives free. He healed the sick, raised the dead, and cast out demons. These works were not exclusive to Him. He was actually modeling the normal Christian life to every believer who would be able to observe His example throughout the centuries to come.

Jesus has empowered us to do the same works He did. At the same time, as we release His will concerning these things through intercession, it is very important that we are mindful of what we *carry*. Jesus very clearly said, "It is finished!" The work was done. Remember, intercession is about enforcing the work of the Cross. Our prayers do not add to or subtract from what Jesus already accomplished. Rather, they must agree with His finished work and release it over the situations of life that need transformation.

Intercessors carry solutions and answers—not burdens and sorrows.

Back to the subject of what we carry. As intercessors, it is important for us to recognize that we carry solutions and answers, *not* emotional burdens, sorrows, and weariness. I am not denying the reality of these feelings, and I am certainly not saying that they are forbidden. I am saying, however, that how intercession has been handled in the past, in some arenas, has been somewhat unhealthy because rather than carrying Heaven's solution—the finished work of Jesus—it was as if the intercessors were taking on the pain and burden of the person or situation they were praying for, as if carrying those feelings would somehow motivate God's response in that matter.

I pray this change in our approach brings freedom and liberty to those who have been trapped in that mindset. We are devoting this entire section to Jesus because we cannot move past Him and His work at Calvary in intercession. The moment we look beyond Him is the moment we start carrying things that have already been carried to the Cross.

Daily Reflection Questions

1. Why is it important to be grounded in the finished work of Jesus to be an effective intercessor?

_____

_____

_____

2. What does it mean to *carry* something in prayer or intercession?

_____

_____

_____

_____

3. In what ways have you carried certain feelings or emotions as an intercessor? How did these emotions help or hinder your prayers?

_____

_____

_____

_____

Daily Meditation

Jesus' finished work on Calvary is the foundation for how we approach intercession. Instead of carrying burdens or heaviness, we carry solutions.

Prayer

Thank You, Father, that the work of Calvary is finished! There is nothing my prayers can do to add or subtract to what Jesus already did, and what He already carried. He carried every burden and weight with Him to the Cross so I could carry His solutions to a world in need of Your Kingdom.
In Jesus' name,
Amen!

For Additional Study

- Read *The Happy Intercessor*, pages 78-79.

- Read *The Joy of Intercession* devotional, pages 99-102.

THE JOY OF HEAVEN RELEASED ON EARTH

...in Your presence is fullness of joy; in Your right hand there are pleasures forever (Psalm 16:11).

All of Heaven is joy! I am not surprised that Jesus carried such joy with Him into the earth, since the world He came from—Heaven—was full of joy. This is why we experience joy when we experience the presence of the Lord here on earth. When His world comes into our world, the climate that defines that world impacts this one. This is such an important reality for intercessors to be aware of.

If we are ambassadors and representatives of God, as Apostle Paul describes in Second Corinthians 5:20, then we need to accurately represent His Kingdom and His world to this one. This means that we live from Heaven to earth. In other words, we live *from* joy. In order to understand this better, we need to continue our study of Jesus.

We cannot allow the circumstances and problems that weigh down this world to weigh on us. Why? It is our responsibility to model Jesus. He was the Man who came from Heaven, the realm of joy; and rather than being moved by the problems He confronted while walking the earth, it was Heaven's joy that moved Him to respond *as the Father would*. As intercessors, we need to do the same thing. I've talked about the tendency for us to carry burdens and weights that Jesus already took.

SHAKE OFF THAT STUFF AND DO WHAT JESUS DID FROM A JOYFUL HEAVEN!

Sometimes, we let the problems that we are called to *pray into* depress us. They fill us with fear, dread, or sorrow. We are overwhelmed with hopelessness, and we think these are right feelings that just come with the turf of intercession. This is not true. These feelings prevent us from releasing power in intercession. Instead of praying solutions, we end up praying the problems—over and over again. It is like our intercession and prayer time become dedicated to making God aware of how big the mountains are and how overwhelming the impossible situations appear to be. It is time to shake that stuff off, and do exactly what Jesus did from the place that Jesus worked—a joyful Heaven!

Jesus was moved with compassion and did God's will. He healed. Raised the dead. Set captives free. If anyone dealt with situations and people who were experiencing the weight of the world, He did. However, He was *never* moved by fear or intimidation. He never allowed the problems He was confronting to get on Him and weigh Him down. He felt. He experienced emotion. He wept over the death of His friend Lazarus. But time after time, we see that Jesus was never swayed by the seriousness or the impossibility of a situation. This allowed Him to boldly speak *into* the darkness and release solutions. Even though we deal with darkness and suffering, we must live like Jesus, from that place of joy, so we are able to boldly offer the world His solutions through our intercession.

Daily Reflection Questions

1. Meditate on Psalm 16:11. How can you experience the joy of Heaven here on earth—as an intercessor?

_____

_____

_____

2. Recall at least three of the miracles that Jesus performed in the Gospels and impossible situations that He solved supernaturally. What was His attitude like and how does this set an example for us on how we should intercede?

    ▪ _____

    ▪ _____

    ▪ _____

3. How can you intercede for the situations in your life—that need supernatural intervention and breakthrough—motivated by *joy?*

    _____

    _____

    _____

    _____

Daily Meditation

Jesus was motivated by the joy of Heaven as He released solutions into suffering and impossibility. As intercessors, we must follow His joyful example instead of becoming consumed by the negative emotions that problems and circumstances carry.

Prayer

> *There is great joy in Your Presence, Father. Thank You for the ability to experience Heaven's joy here on earth as I come into that secret place. As I intercede, I am motivated by this joy. I am joyful because I carry Heaven's supernatural solutions for the problems and suffering in this world.*
> *In Jesus' name,*
> *Amen*

For Additional Study

- Read *The Happy Intercessor*, pages 80-81.

- Read *The Joy of Intercession* devotional, pages 103-106.

THE JOY OF JESUS' MIRACLES

He [Jesus] clasped the girl's hand and said, "Talitha koum," which means, "Little girl, get up." At that, she was up and walking around! This girl was twelve years of age. They, of course, were all beside themselves with joy (Mark 5:41-42 MSG).

To me, the phrase—"they were all beside themselves with joy"—gives us a preview into how Jesus responded to the miraculous. As intercessors, we are equipped with everything we need to experience a lifestyle of breakthrough. The miraculous should be our normal. We are seeing this more and more across the nations. People are running with this idea of a new normal Christian life—the one modeled by Jesus.

As intercessors embrace this charge, we are setting ourselves up to pray into some incredible situations and witness the power of Jesus powerfully turn them around. The important thing to remember is this—while a supernatural lifestyle and the fruit it brings should be normal for us, it can never be common. It can never become same old, same old. Whether He heals cancer or mends a broken finger, we must celebrate the fact that Jesus' joyful Kingdom is breaking into our world.

AS AN INTERCESSOR, THE MIRACULOUS SHOULD BE YOUR NORMAL.

I have to believe this is why Jesus responded to His miracles with such joy. It was not joy that comes from surprise. Jesus knew what He carried and what He offered impossible situations. I believe His joy had everything to do with seeing the world He knew so well, Heaven, touch the world He loved so dearly—earth. In Mark 5, Heaven breaks into a situation as Jesus raises a little girl from the dead. Heaven simply vibrates with life. Death is not known in that world.

Jesus is the Great Intercessor between humankind and God (see Rom. 8:34). In order for us as intercessors to change our countenance and adopt a joyful approach to what we do has everything to do with how we see Jesus. If the Great Intercessor is downtrodden, always serious, and stoic, it only makes sense that we will model this behavior. After all, we are called to be like Jesus. The problem comes when we model something that is inaccurate. Jesus was a man of supernatural joy. In fact, our next lesson—which ends this particular session—is devoted to us having an accurate, joyful vision of Jesus.

For now, let's model Jesus' reaction to the miraculous. Yes, we can even become religious about the supernatural if we do not maintain this joy. I love our friends, John and Carol Arnott. To me, they beautifully model the joy of Jesus, the Miracle Worker. Time after time they witness God do the amazing, and their response is always the same: Wonder. Awe. Joy. Celebration. It never gets old. May it be the same for us!

Daily Reflection Questions

1.   Why do you think Jesus responds to miracles with joy?

_____

_____

_____

_____

2. How can we model Jesus' joy when it comes to intercession and celebrating the prayers that God answers?

_____

_____

_____

_____

3. Why do you think it is important to keep your sense of joy and wonder when it comes to God answering prayer?

_____

_____

_____

_____

Daily Meditation

Jesus responded to the miraculous with joy. In intercession, we follow His example when we always maintain a sense of joy and awe as God answers prayer. It never gets old!

Prayer

Lord, help me to keep a sense of joy and wonder—every single time You answer prayer. May I celebrate all of Your works and respond to them just like Jesus did, with outrageous joy. How wonderful are Your works, Father. Each one reveals a greater glimpse of who You are.
In Jesus' name,
Amen

For Additional Study

▪ Read *The Happy Intercessor*, pages 81-83.

Day Five

THE INCOMPARABLE
JOY OF KING JESUS

*But to the Son He says…"Therefore God, Your God,
has anointed You With the oil of gladness more
than Your companions"* (Hebrews 1:8-9).

As we wrap up this section about Jesus, *the* Happy Intercessor, I want us to get a clear picture of what this looks like. Our joy in intercession comes from understanding what we have learned so far about Jesus, that:

- He joyfully participated in God's redemptive plan as He knew the fruit that it was going to produce.

- His work on Calvary is finished, giving us the ability to carry solutions not burdens.

- He was strengthened by the joy of Heaven and released it on earth.

- He rejoiced over His miracles because they are expressions of the joyful world of Heaven defeating sorrow and suffering.

We have so far studied the joyful works of Jesus because they give you and me examples of how to joyfully engage in intercession. However, it does not take long to study Jesus' works before we are invited into experiencing His heart and His nature.

Hebrews 1:8 and 9 paint such a beautiful picture of a Jesus who simply radiated joy. The New Living Translation describes Jesus as having received *the oil of joy...more than anyone else.* In other words, Jesus exuded joy that was incomparable.

INTERCESSION STARTS AND ENDS WITH A VISION OF JOY.

When I think of a joyful Jesus, I think of the scene in the movie *Passion of the Christ,* where Jesus is at home, and He is building a table. His mother comes out and they start laughing together. Even though I know that is something the writer added to the movie, I have to imagine that is how Jesus lived. Again, Scripture tells us that He was anointed with the oil of gladness more than His companions. When it came to people who experienced and expressed joy, Jesus stood out above the rest! As intercessors following His model, may it be said of us that our joy stands out among the rest. After all, we get to work with Jesus in seeing His plans come to pass in the earth.

I end with painting this simple picture of a joyful Jesus because intercession starts and ends with a vision of joy. It begins with understanding that our Advocate, Christ Jesus, the One who ever makes intercession, is full of joy. It ends with God's joyful Kingdom breaking into this world, destroying darkness, relieving suffering, and transforming impossible situations.

Reflection Questions

1. Read Hebrews 1:8-9. What does a *joyful* Jesus look like to you and how does this agree/conflict with images you have had of Jesus?

_____

_____

2. Why is a vision of a joyful Jesus important for you to effectively in-
    tercede and experience God's Kingdom breaking into this world?

_____

_____

_____

3. Why do you think Jesus was so joyful, even though He dealt with
    suffering and ultimately would have to suffer Himself?

_____

_____

_____

Daily Meditation

A key to our intercession bearing fruit and releasing the Kingdom is
having a clear vision of a joyful Jesus.

Prayer

> *Give me eyes to see Jesus as He truly is—the Man filled with joy
> more than anyone else. Open my eyes to the joy of Jesus through-
> out the Word. As I intercede, help me to keep my eyes fixed on
> Jesus, the Happy Intercessor. Lord, You are joyful because You love
> me, and You are joyful because we get to work together to see Your
> Kingdom change this world.*
> *In Jesus' name,*
> *Amen*

For Additional Study

- Read *The Joy of Intercession* devotional, pages 103-106.

UNLOCKING THE THREE REALMS THROUGH INTERCESSION

"I've discovered that there are many intercessors who do not live out of a place of joy because they get stuck in the first or second realms. When intercessors get stuck in the first realm, they get preoccupied with logic and reason. Then their prayers become focused on what *seems logical,* which is not where God is coming from most of the time! And then there are those intercessors who get stuck in the second realm. This realm is the dark and demonic realm, which produces hopelessness, doom, and fear. Instead, we need to make sure that we remain focused on God and what He is doing. The key is to always ask God, "Father, what are You doing?"

—BENI JOHNSON

Session 4

Unlocking the Three Realms through Intercession

Discussion Questions

The first realm contains the _____ and _____.

The second realm contains _____ and _____ activity and warfare.

The third realm is the _____ realm of God's Presence.

Informed Intercession = Seeing into the second realm so we are equipped to _____ more effectively.

We need to intercede and prophesy from the _____ realm; this is God's perspective.

Benefits of Praying from the Third Realm:

Benefit 1: God's _____ gives us His perspective in prayer.

Benefit 2: It will _____ our prayers and release transformation to the other two realms.

Day One

DEFINING THE THREE REALMS

The word realm means "source" or "on each side."

*I*ntercessors have the ability to pick up on many things that are going on in the spirit realm. This comes with the territory. The problem is that many remain stuck in a realm that they are not designed to live from.

Here's the deal, often times it seems like intercessors get so focused on the negative—what the devil is up to and what he is doing—that they don't look to what God is doing. We must feed ourselves on the works of the Lord. This is what nourishes our intercession.

Junk food does nothing for our bodies. In fact, it does the very opposite of foods that we consider healthy. While there are certain foods that build us up, providing our bodies with nutrients and nourishment, there are also foods that break our bodies down. They hurt, rather than help. There is no neutral zone here. It's not like eating junk food does nothing. We would not be experiencing the widespread crisis in health that we are today if eating junk food carried no impact. But it does. It carries a strong negative impact, and the same is true in the spirit realm when we live from the wrong place.

What you feed on as an intercessor will determine your focus in prayer. What we feed or focus on has everything to do with which of the three realms we are living out of. That is why I am devoting these next five days to this topic, as well as a full video session. For us to carry power and effectiveness in our intercession, we need to identify what realm we are living out of, and if need be, make the needed adjustments.

What you feed on as an intercessor determines your focus in prayer.

As I mentioned at the beginning, there are many intercessors who get stuck living out of the demonic realm where they end up spending the majority of their focus on the enemy and his strategies. The only reason the enemy's strategies are revealed to us are so we can break them and release God's supernatural solutions over them! By focusing all of our attention on the enemy, we are actually agreeing with his plans and strategies, and this agreement is exactly how we give him power.

Again, as intercessors we *will* pick up on things that are taking place in the demonic realm. This is normal. In fact, this is what gives us the upper hand advantage to witness the miraculous; for as intercessors, we carry the power to break the enemy's strategies and destroy his works by enforcing the work of Jesus. The key for us is to live from the right place so that we impact darkness rather than darkness impacting us.

Daily Reflection Questions

1. Why is it important to be aware of the realm from which you live your spiritual life? (Especially if there are both healthy and unhealthy spiritual realms.)

_____

_____

_____

_____

2. How do you think the spiritual realm you *live from* impacts the position that you *pray from?*

    _____

    _____

    _____

    _____

3. Before you go on to study the topic further in the pages to come, can you recall any personal experiences you have had with different spiritual realms?

    _____

    _____

    _____

    _____

4. Using your experience(s) as a guidepost, what do you think it means to live out of a particular spiritual realm, and how would this impact the course of someone's spiritual life?

    _____

    _____

    _____

    _____

Daily Meditation

It is important that we recognize in which of the three spiritual realms we spend the most time, as this helps us evaluate why our intercession is either effective or ineffective. The spiritual realm that we live from impacts everything, especially how we pray!

Prayer

Lord, I recognize that this is an important subject. Renew my mind over the days to come. Increase my understanding. Fill me with the spirit of wisdom and revelation in the knowledge of You. Open my eyes to know which spiritual realm I am living from, give me clarity on how that place is impacting the way I pray, and empower me to make the needed changes to step into a position of intimacy and victory.

In Jesus' name,

Amen

For Additional Study

- Read *The Happy Intercessor*, pages 91-92.

- Read *The Joy of Intercession* devotional, pages 107-110.

Day Two

THE FIRST REALM: PHYSICAL AND VISIBLE

Now I saw a new heaven and a new earth, for the first heaven and the first earth had passed away… (Revelation 21:1).

The first realm is the natural or physical realm—the realm you can see with your natural eyes. In Revelation 21:1, we see that the first heaven is the earthly realm. In Deuteronomy 10:14 (NASB), we see that *"to the Lord your God belong heaven and the highest heavens, the earth and all that is in it."* According to the *New American Standard Exhaustive Concordance* of the Bible, the word *heaven* means "astrologers, compass, Earth, heaven, heavens." This includes the atmosphere, sky, and space, along with the earth.

This is the realm we presently see with our eyes and live in. Note, however, that I use the phrase "live in," and not *life from*. As we study these realms in depth, this is such an important difference to note. For intercessors, interaction with each realm is going to happen. It's unavoidable. What we need to learn is how to live from the right realm so that we can impact the other ones. It goes without saying that we have been anointed, empowered, and commissioned to make an impact on the first realm—the realm we presently live in and occupy on planet Earth.

YOU MUST BE GROUNDED IN THE RIGHT REALM TO SUPERNATURALLY IMPACT PLANET EARTH.

Our bodies, our homes, and our cities exist in this earthly first realm. Again, this is everything we can see right now. God has a clear will for each of these things, which is summed up in Matthew 6:10, *on earth as it is in heaven*. Everything that we currently see and interact with in the earthly realm is destined to be transformed by God's realm, Heaven. He has a very specific plan for our bodies, our homes, and our cities, namely that His glory will fill every arena of this earthly realm starting with those things. As intercessors, we have parts to play in seeing God's glory, the currency of His realm (Heaven), impact this first natural realm.

The Lord's Prayer actually gives us a glimpse of how the realms are supposed to work and interact with each other, specifically the third realm (Heaven)—which we are going to study in the days ahead—and the first realm (first earth, physical). To make this as uncomplicated as possible, we must be rooted and grounded in the right realm in order to release supernatural impact, or a heavenly impact, on this first realm, planet Earth.

In conclusion, the first realm is not the place you and I have been redeemed to live from. The proof is in the Person who lives inside of us, the Holy Spirit. God has filled us with His own Presence; yes for empowerment for service, but also to enable us to live from His heavenly realm. Only the Holy Spirit can help us do this, for He has personal experience in that realm. It is His point of origin. In Jesus' baptism and on the Day of Pentecost, we see evidence of this as the Spirit was released from one realm to the next, from the third realm (Heaven) to the first realm (earth).

Daily Reflection Questions

1. Based on what you have just read, how would you describe the *first realm?*

_____

_____

_____

2. In the book *The Happy Intercessor*, Beni wrote that "when intercessors get stuck in the first realm, they get preoccupied with logic and reason. Then their prayers become focused on what seems logical, which is not where God is coming from most of the time." How does getting stuck in the first realm rob your intercession of its power?

_____

_____

_____

_____

3. As an intercessor, what impact should you be having on the first realm through intercession?

_____

_____

_____

_____

Daily Meditation

The first realm—the world we can see with our natural eyes—is not the realm we are designed to live from; but rather, it is the realm we are empowered to transform through intercession.

Prayer

Father, show me how to live in this world, but not be of it. I am an ambassador of Your world. I am a representative of Jesus in the earth. Heaven is my home, not just after I die, but right now. This is the realm I have been saved to live from. I am called and empowered to bring Your realm to this one through intercession and see natural things transformed by Your supernatural power. In Jesus' name, Amen

For Additional Study

- Read *The Happy Intercessor*, pages 91-92.

- Read *The Joy of Intercession* devotional, pages 107-108.

THE SECOND REALM: DEMONIC AND ANGELIC ACTIVITY

And I saw another angel flying in midheaven,
having an eternal gospel to preach to those who live
on the earth, and to every nation and tribe and
tongue and people (Revelation 14:6 NASB).

*T*he second heaven, or mid-heaven, is the demonic and angelic realm where there is war going on between two opposing kingdoms. This is the realm where spiritual warfare takes place—and unfortunately, the place where too many intercessors have gotten stuck. While we do battle in this realm, we have not been designed to live from it. The second realm is not our home, just as the first realm is not. In the same way we are not supposed to conform to the ways of the world—the first realm— we are not supposed to become stuck in the second realm.

I have discovered that intercessors who do not live out of a place of joy are this way because they get stuck in the first or second realms. In particular, being stuck in the second realm really drains the life and joy out of intercessors, as they become overly consumed with what the devil is doing. The second realm is the zone of his operation.

This is also the realm that is accessed through the discerning of spirits. Remember, the gifts of the Holy Spirit as listed in First Corinthians 12 are to edify the Body of Christ. No one is edified by people who misunderstand discernment as their license to live in a realm of warfare. I assure you, this is not a healthy thing. All you are doing is setting yourself up for a burdensome spiritual life that can ultimately lead to hopelessness, doom, and fear.

Do not give the enemy the pleasure of your time.

When you become stuck in the second realm, you end up praying from a defensive place, not an offensive one as we had studied previously. Remember, the fight is fixed. Calvary won the victory. Even though we know that, being stuck in the second realm—where we are inundated with demonic activity—has the ability to steal our vision. Our eyes should be fixed on the victorious Christ and a Cross that completely dismantled the devil and wrecked his house of cards. It is a fact that focus is very powerful. What we look at the most becomes the thing that drives our prayer life. It goes without saying that when all we see are destructive strategies, demonic presences, and darkness, our intercession perspective shifts and prayer becomes something we use to chase the devil around with.

This is what it looks like. You are watching TV or reading the newspaper and some bad news comes up. You have just been made aware of the first realm. You become defensive and start praying on a human level, as you experience fear. The other option is you see into the demonic realm. Sometimes it feels like pressure, like you have to pray *now*, and if you don't, the entire world will unravel and collapse. This begins the chase the enemy wants to consume you with, where you start investing your intercession into him. Let's not give him the pleasure of our time. His realm is not the focus of the place of intercession. If anything, his realm is severely impacted when we live and pray from the right realm. This is what we will study next.

Daily Reflection Questions

1. What does it look like to live and pray from the second realm?

_____

_____

_____

2. How does praying from the second realm keep you on the defensive and distract you from focusing on the finished work of the Cross?

_____

_____

_____

3. Why do you think the enemy tries to get intercessors stuck living from the second realm?

_____

_____

4. What are some ways you can avoid falling into this trap?

_____

_____

_____

Daily Meditation

The second realm—where demonic and angelic activity takes place—can be engaged through intercession, but cannot be the place where intercessors spend most of their time. This puts us on the defensive, running after the devil, instead of the offensive—releasing God's will and strategies into the earth.

Prayer

Father, I desire to release Your light into the darkness. Help me to not focus on the works of the enemy and his strategies. If I am exposed to any of his strategies through discernment or revelation, help me to pray Your solutions, thwarting his plans of evil. Jesus was sent to destroy the works of the devil, not spend His lifetime focused on them. Help me to follow that example and enforce the victorious work of Calvary through intercession!

In Jesus' name,

Amen

For Additional Study

- Read *The Happy Intercessor*, pages 92-95.

- Read *The Joy of Intercession* devotional, page 110.

THE THIRD REALM: GOD'S GLORIOUS PRESENCE

[God] raised us up with Him [Christ], and seated us with Him in the heavenly places in Christ Jesus (Ephesians 2:6).

Today, I am going to describe the third realm, and then tomorrow, we are going to study what it means to live from this place and, in turn, transform the other realms through intercession. The third realm is the realm where the glory of God dwells.

It is in His glory where we experience true transformation and change into the image of Jesus (see 2 Cor. 3:18). As we are going to study, living from the third realm—the place of God's Presence—enables us to see every other realm transformed by His power and Kingdom. Our position is being seated with Christ in heavenly places, even though we live on earth. In order to see the other realms transformed, we need to live in the glorious realm of Heaven...while we walk on earth.

The third realm is where every believer should live. You see, all believers should live and intercede from the place of victory, knowing and partnering with the strategies of God. You become exposed to His ways, His will, and His plans as you spend time in His glorious presence. Because of Jesus' blood, you have been granted unrestricted access to the Presence of God *right now*. The very presence that was hidden behind a veil for centuries is now available for our experience and enjoyment.

This is amazing and as intercessors, His Presence is the world we must be consumed by.

You are seated with Christ in heavenly places...now.

In Second Corinthians 12:2-4, Paul was in this place and wrote how he was *"caught up into Paradise and heard inexpressible words."* Paul was given a vision of the actual place called Heaven. This is the third realm. At the same time, even though we are not bodily present in Heaven, we are described as citizens of this place. As mentioned before, Paul actually says we are seated with Christ in heavenly places...*now.*

Visions and spiritual experiences of Heaven are increasing in the Body of Christ. This is definitely a way for us to grasp what His realm is like so we can more effectively live from it. At the same time, the very climate and culture of Heaven is defined by Him and His Presence. To be in the Presence of God is to essentially experience Heaven on earth. We cannot misunderstand, however. There is the full expression of an actual place called Heaven that waits for us after we leave this life. Also, God continues to give His children access to that place now through visions and supernatural experiences. In addition we are given insight into the third realm as we experience His Presence.

Daily Reflection Questions

1.   What are some ways can you access the third realm today?

_____

_____

_____

_____

_____

2. How are you transformed in the Presence of the Lord? (Read Second Corinthians 3:18.)

    _____

    _____

    _____

3. List some ways you have personally experienced the third realm of God's glory. How did these experiences impact your prayer life?

    _____

    _____

    _____

Daily Meditation

The third realm is the place where God's glorious presence dwells. The Presence must be the place we devote most attention to if we want to joyfully release God's will into the earth through intercession.

Prayer

> *Father, may Your Presence consume my focus and pursuit. Thank You for the blood of Jesus that made a way for me to experience Your glory now. Reveal Your plans and purposes to me as I simply enjoy being with You. There is nowhere else I'd rather be than with You, in Your glory, hearing Your heartbeat and being transformed into the image of Your Son.*
> *In Jesus' name,*
> *Amen*

For Additional Study

- Read *The Happy Intercessor*, page 93.

- Read *The Joy of Intercession* devotional, pages 115-118.

LIVING FROM THE THIRD REALM, TRANSFORMING THE OTHERS

*For all have sinned and fall short of the
glory of God* (Roman 3:23).

Because of Jesus' work, we have been restored to the place that we fell away from because of sin—the glory. This is the realm we were designed to live from and as intercessors, this is the realm that we need to pray from. This is the third ream that we talked about yesterday. Today, we are going to take the spiritual and make it practical by applying it to our everyday lives.

This third realm is the place where we step into our identity as people seated with Christ in heavenly places. When we have clear focus on what His world looks like, we have a vision of the realm we are designed to live and intercede from.

There are many who try to pray and intercede from the first and second realms. Intercession from the first realm focuses on natural solutions, when in fact God is a supernatural being who specializes in bringing supernatural answers. Intercession from the second realm focuses on the darkness and demonic realm, spending most of its time dealing with the devil. We have studied the differences between the three realms this week, but the key difference is that by living from and interceding from the third realm, we actually release solutions rather than focusing on circumstances and problems.

Fear-based prayers carry no solutions and produce no heavenly answers.

Being focused on the first and second realm brings us away from that third realm and keeps us focused on the devil or the things in life that trouble us. When we intercede or prophesy out of the first two realms, we are not praying according to Heaven. Most of the time, we are praying out of fear—fear of the hopeless situation or fear of the devil. The prayers that are fear-based are not prayers that will carry a solution; and in turn, they will not produce a heavenly answer.

Can we know what is going on in those first two realms, or should we completely ignore them? It's definitely OK to be aware of what is taking place in those realms. We need to be aware of what is happening in the first realm, as that is the realm we have the most interaction with. To separate from that is to separate from natural reality. Even a healthy attention is OK when it comes to the second realm, as it makes us more informed with our prayers. It's informational, as we see what spiritual forces are motivating different people and situations. Knowledge of the first two realms is information and fuel, but anything beyond that needs to be avoided. We cannot live and pray out of those realms.

Remember, Jesus has redeemed us and positioned us to live in the glory of God. This is the realm we need to live and pray out of. That type of lifestyle is offensive and releases spiritual power. Why? We remain focused on what the Father is doing. We ask, "Father, show me what You are doing." He responds, and we then model Jesus. We say what the Father is saying, and we do what He is doing in response to the first two realms.

Daily Reflection Questions

1. What happens when you start praying from the first or second realms?

    ▪ Results of praying from the first realm:

    _____

    _____

    _____

    ▪ Results of praying from the second realm:

    _____

    _____

    _____

2. How have you interacted with the first realm and the second realm in the past?

    _____

    _____

    _____

3. How is God calling you to live and pray from the third realm?

    _____

    _____

    _____

Daily Meditation

Effective prayer and intercession takes place when we live from the third realm—praying out of God's presence and glory. When He is our focus, not circumstances or the devil, our prayers come into alignment with the heartbeat of heaven and release Kingdom solutions.

Prayer

Father, take me into greater depths of intimacy with You. Help me to not become consumed with everything that is going on around me that needs a solution. Also, help me not to become distracted by the enemy and spend time focusing on his strategies. Show me how to say what You are saying, and pray the things that are on Your heart. Your words are spirit and they are life. Help me to live in Your Presence so that the words I speak would carry Your Presence, Your word, and Your life into the situations that need breakthrough.
In Jesus' name,
Amen

For Additional Study

- Read *The Happy Intercessor*, pages 96-100.

PRINCIPLES FOR PRAYER THAT DIRECT SPIRITUAL AIRWAYS

"Those who own the airways control the atmosphere. The *airways* are the spiritual climate over a city. It is our responsibility to take ownership of the airways and reclaim the atmosphere. When we do that, a shift takes place in the spiritual climate in the region. When that shift takes place, we begin to see signs of revival, and entire cities become transformed by the things of God. When cities become transformed by the things of God, we see more light and less darkness in entire regions."

—BENI JOHNSON

Session 5

PRINCIPLES FOR PRAYER THAT DIRECT SPIRITUAL AIRWAYS

DISCUSSION QUESTIONS

Those who take the airways own the
_____.

Your intercession causes a _____ in atmospheres of darkness.

All matter has _____.

You carry God's _____, which changes the atmosphere.

Your intercession _____ with God's decision-making process.

Day One

OWN THE AIRWAYS, CONTROL THE ATMOSPHERE

...The earnest (heartfelt, continued) prayer of a
righteous man makes tremendous power available
[dynamic in its working] (James 5:16 AMP).

As intercessors, we have a unique responsibility for our cities and regions. You are not where you are by accident; God has positioned you there for such a time as this! I am not saying you will never leave and you are assigned to be there forever. However, while you live in a certain city, you as an intercessor have the ability to make an investment in the spiritual soil of that geography. Through your prayers and intercession, you have the ability to actually help direct the atmosphere of that entire region!

In the days to come, we are going to be discussing *airways*. To make it simple, airways represent the spiritual climates over cities. When we take authority and ownership over these airways, a shift takes place in the spiritual climate over these regions. When this shift takes place, we start to see signs of revival. Before long, entire cities are transformed by the Kingdom of God. When we study the great moves of God throughout history, without fail, we witness intercessors working behind the scenes to help direct the spiritual atmosphere being released over a city or region.

I cannot help but think of John Nelson Hyde, often referred to as *Praying Hyde*. As he experienced tremendous regional breakthrough and revival in the early 1900s, it is amazing to note where the victory was actually won. While thousands of lives were publicly impacted by the presence of God, Hyde and a few others interceded in private.

Your prayers are powerful and dynamic.

Even though intercession takes place in the "background," what happens in the secret place has a tremendous effect on what we see in public. Hyde's private intercession birthed a very public revival. It is so important that we get it. I know "intercessory prayer" has been looked at as something that people do "off hours." Whether it happens off hours, in a closet, or in your car, I want to encourage you, what happens in that secret place possesses the power to control atmospheres over entire cities and geographies. James 5:16 makes it clear. Your prayers are powerful and *dynamic* in their working!

It's time we open our eyes to the public power we release through private intercession. I believe if we really understood what we have been given access to in this gift of intercession, not only would every believer be engaged in this ministry, but we would be witnessing significant spiritual shifts in cities around the earth. We're getting there, though! What's held us back is the very thing we are learning to press through in this series.

For too long, intercession has been misunderstood. As a result, believers have been unwilling to take their place as intercessors. I totally understand. I didn't want to be part of it either...until the Lord really opened my eyes to what intercession is, and what it truly does.

Daily Reflection Questions

1. Read James 5:16. What would happen if we started to actually believe that our intercession contained the power to impact entire cities and regions? How would this change your approach to prayer and intercession?

2. What reservations have you had (either currently, or in the past) about becoming an intercessor?

3. What do you think would happen if all believers took their places as intercessors and began to take spiritual ownership over their cities?

Daily Meditation

When believers recognize that their private intercessions contain and carry the power to release breakthrough over entire regions, this ministry no longer becomes optional—it becomes essential!

Prayer

Lord, I thank You that because of the blood of Jesus Christ, I am righteous. That is my status in Him! Because of this, I come into agreement with James 5:16. Because I am righteous, my prayers contain and release dynamic power. Open my eyes to what intercession possesses the power to do over my city. Show me how to effectively invest into my region through prayer and intercession, so that I get to celebrate in the breakthrough and spiritual shift that takes place.
In Jesus' name,
Amen

For Additional Study

- Read *The Happy Intercessor*, pages 101-103.

- Read *The Joy of Intercession* devotional, pages 119-122.

Day Two

WAR IN THE HEAVENLIES

...I have come in response to your words. But the
prince of the kingdom of Persia was withstanding
me for twenty-one days... (Daniel 10:12-13).

Our understanding of airways, spiritual atmospheres, and the three realms (we studied about last week) all work together. Let me illustrate using an example in Daniel's life.

Daniel knew something about dealing with spiritual atmospheres over regions and cities. He had received a message, but needed understanding of the message. He went on to fast for twenty-one days. At the end of the twenty-one days, an angel came and told him that he had come because of Daniel's prayers. That said, there was a struggle between this angel and the ruling demonic forces over a region. It actually took Michael, the warring angel, to come and fight this prince of Persia.

Even though the angel was sent at the very beginning of Daniel's fast, it took twenty-one days for the message to get through with the help of Michael. The Kingdom always prevails over darkness. However, there was an element of persistence and perseverance required from Daniel's part to co-labor with the angelic forces that were engaged in combat with the demonic forces over Persia.

Daniel was engaged in warfare in the second realm. Remember, this is the realm of the invisible world—where we are given sight into the demonic and angelic worlds. This tends to be a place that so allures and captures the intercessor that, sadly, they end up getting stuck there, focused on the combat.

DARKNESS DOES NOT STAND A CHANCE AGAINST THE ARMIES OF THE LIVING GOD.

Get this. When we live in that third realm of God's glory and presence, there is no combat. How can this be? What about the struggle between Michael the angel and the demonic prince of Persia? Even though warfare is transpiring, the fight is fixed. Third realm perspective grounds us in the secured victory. Darkness does not stand a chance when dealing with the armies of the Living God. Even though this is true, you can see how someone who is so focused on the struggle in the second realm would quickly lose that perspective of victory.

The key is modeling Daniel. He experienced breakthrough and victory over these regional principalities because he was a man of the third realm. In other words, his focus was fixed on what God was doing instead of what the demonic forces were doing, preventing, or trying to destroy. He obviously was not ignorant of the conflict. But he knew just enough to become a more effective intercessor.

Let's follow this example as we pray over our cities and regions. Are there powers at work that require angelic combat? Yes. The key is remembering that we pray *from* victory and we must keep our eyes fixed on the Victorious One.

Daily Reflection Questions

1. Read Daniel 10:10-14. Why is it so important to be focused on the third realm of God's presence and glory when dealing with spiritual combat?

   _____

   _____

   _____

2. How does praying *from the place of victory* empower us to intercede for our cities and regions, no matter how ungodly the people, culture, or systems seem to be?

   _____

   _____

   _____

3. In what ways is God calling you to intercede for your city and region? Ask the Holy Spirit to reveal specific things, people, or places that you can intercede for. Write them in the spaces below:

   - _____

   - _____

   - _____

   - _____

Daily Meditation

To experience victory in spiritual combat, the key is keeping focused on the third realm—the place of God's presence and glory. Even though there is warfare going on in the second realm, between angelic and demonic forces, the fight is fixed. Our intercession simply enforces what has already been secured and releases it over cities and regions.

Prayer

Father, lift my eyes. Help me to not focus on the combat going on between angels and demons. Even though there is warfare going on, I'm grateful that victory has already been purchased. Principalities and powers have been disarmed. Darkness has been defeated. Thank You, Lord, for winning ALL of it at Calvary. Show me how to enforce these truths through intercession as I pray for cities and regions.
In Jesus' name,
Amen

For Additional Study:

- Read *The Happy Intercessor*, pages 103-104.

- Read *The Joy of Intercession* devotional, pages 123-126.

Day Three

HOW TO REACT WHEN CHANGE COMES

*Hope deferred makes the heart sick, but desire fulfilled
is a tree of life* (Proverbs 13:12 NASB).

One of the sure signs that your prayers are in agreement with Heaven is that you will begin to see changes. I encourage you—don't just look for the big and obvious. Small shifts are just as important as sudden turnarounds. Why? Both reveal how powerful our intercession is in changing the atmosphere and directing the airways.

So many people end up giving up before experiencing the full release of breakthrough. Perseverance is quickly becoming a foreign concept to us in our fast-food society. The idea of having to wait for anything actually draws people away from intercession. Oftentimes we have the opportunity to experience immediate results when we pray for healing or deliverance. Of course, this is not all of the time. However, the fact remains that those who pray for breakthrough in healing and deliverance tend to experience faster results than intercessors who are agreeing with Heaven to see shifts over regions and nations.

**INTERCESSORS MUST STOP, OBSERVE, AND OFFER
UP THANKSGIVING TO AVOID BURNOUT.**

We must remember that the same God who opens blind eyes and deaf ears is the same God who breaks into nations and brings salvation to entire regions. Though the task appears great—bringing change to nations—the truth is we must celebrate every single shift as a significant breakthrough. When righteous laws are passed, celebrate. When immorality is on the decline, offer thanks. When the entertainment industry recognizes the need to produce high-quality, faith-based content, shift is taking place.

The problem happens when we as intercessors do not stop, observe, and offer up thanksgiving. It is so easy for us to develop such an intense momentum in prayer and intercession that we keep contending, and crying, and calling forth—when in fact, things are already starting to happen. Our intercession is producing fruit. When we don't stop to offer God thanks for what He is doing, regardless how small it appears, we position ourselves for intercession burnout.

This is how we must respond when the changes start to take place. At Bethel, Proverbs 13:12 is a verse you will hear quoted often. It makes such a simple, powerful truth, which the Message Bible brings some interesting emphasis to—especially relating to intercession: "*Unrelenting disappointment leaves you heartsick, but a sudden good break can turn life around.*"

Let us not be intercessors who experience unrelenting disappointment. This is very possible when we live in the first and second realms, focused on all the problems, hopelessness, demonic influences, principalities, etc. Intercession is our weapon to solve these problems; celebrate every shift that takes place! Regardless how large or small our *sudden good breaks* appear to be, when our hearts are set to celebrate them, our prayer *life* will *turn around* quickly.

Daily Reflection Questions

1. Why is it so important to celebrate and offer thanksgiving when change starts taking place—regardless how big or small?

   _____

   _____

   _____

   _____

2. What tends to happen when we keep moving forward in intercession, not paying attention to the things God is actually doing?

   _____

   _____

   _____

   _____

3. Review the four things you committed to pray and intercede for yesterday. What positive shifts and changes do you see happening in each of those areas?

   - _____

   - _____

   - _____

   - _____

Daily Meditation

When the focus is on what is not happening, intercession becomes grueling spiritual toil. However, when people stop and focus on what shifts their prayers are producing, intercession becomes empowered and energized by fresh faith.

Prayer

Holy Spirit, show me how You are moving. Help me to stop and focus on what You are doing, and give You thanks and praise for the shifts that are taking place. Lord, I know that whether they are large or small, any shift, any change, any breakthrough is worth celebrating. It reminds me of the power of prayer and intercession. Thank You, Father, for building my faith as I stop to focus on what You are doing and how You are moving. In Jesus' name,
Amen

For Additional Study

- Read *The Happy Intercessor*, pages 105-108.

STANDING IN THE GAP

I searched for a man among them who would build up the wall and stand in the gap before Me for the land, so that I would not destroy it; but I found no one (Ezekiel 22:30 NASB).

When it comes to intercession, Ezekiel 22:30 is one of those key verses that many of us reference. To me, it is a wonderful challenge. It's asking, "What are you waiting for?" This Scripture gives you and me the right to stand up and say to God, "Here I am! I'll do it. I'll be the one who stands. I'll take my place as the wall You're looking for!"

I don't want God wondering why there is no intercessor. Rather, I want Him to be satisfied with what He sees in me and sees in you. What an amazing calling it is for us to stand in "the gap" and have a transformative, influential voice before the throne of God. Again, I am convinced that the only reason we do not pursue intercession more is because we are not fully clued in to its power. We actually have a voice before the throne of God. Perhaps under the Old Covenant, such a position was only for the priests or the prophets. Not the case now. Because of Jesus, we have the ability to *"draw near with confidence to the throne of grace"* (Heb. 4:16).

The only reason we do not joyfully embrace the challenge to stand in the gap is because we need a confidence boost. We must believe that our voices, standing in agreement with the Father's heart and the voice of the Great Intercessor, Jesus, actually make a difference. Like I said, the invitation has been given to every believer. Just as we have been redeemed and given access to the Presence of God, we have been cleared to enter boldly before His throne and offer up intercession on behalf of those who are voiceless.

> **YOUR INTERCESSIONS ON BEHALF OF THE VOICELESS ALLOWS YOU TO EXPERIENCE INCREDIBLE BREAKTHROUGHS.**

This is why we "stand in the gap." There are so many people who have not yet encountered the Father. As a result, they are voiceless before His throne. This is not to say that Heaven does not hear their cries. What I am saying is that there are so many people out there—even among friends and family—who don't even know they are able to come to the Father. They don't know that, because of Jesus, they have access and permission to enter His Presence with boldness, to make known their requests and petitions, and to *receive mercy and find grace to help in time of need"* (Heb. 4:16).

Because of this, we must embrace this wonderful challenge and opportunity. You and I have the ability to offer our voices in intercession on behalf of those who do not. Because of your intercessions on behalf of the voiceless, you get to participate in some of the most incredible breakthroughs imaginable. As those who don't have a relationship with God experience supernatural results because of those who are interceding, it is their invitation to transition from orphan to beloved child of the Father.

Daily Reflection Questions

1. What does it mean to "Stand in the gap," and how does it relate to intercession?

    _____

    _____

    _____

2. How does your voice make a difference on behalf of those who don't have a voice before God?

    _____

    _____

    _____

3. What does it mean to have a "voice before the throne" as opposed to being one who is "voiceless?"

    _____

    _____

    _____

4. Who are you standing in the gap for in your life—being a voice on their behalf before the throne of God?

    _____

    _____

    _____

    Note: Be sure to persevere in intercession for these people. Remember, even the smallest shifts are worth your celebration as they are signs pointing to impending breakthrough in their lives.

Daily Meditation

Intercessors are assigned to be voices before the throne of God in prayer, on behalf of those who are not bringing their petitions and requests to Him.

Prayer

> *Father, open my eyes to the power of my voice before Your throne. Thank You for Your grace and mercy that gives me the ability to stand in Your presence and to boldly make intercession on behalf of those who don't know You yet. I pray that I would celebrate both the big and small breakthroughs with them, so that they would more and more see Your goodness at work in their lives, which draws them to You.*
> *In Jesus' name,*
> *Amen*

For Additional Study:

- Read *The Happy Intercessor*, pages 112-114.

INTERCESSION: THE LANGUAGE OF FRIENDSHIP

No longer do I call you servants, for a servant
does not know what his master is doing; but I
have called you friends... (John 15:15).

This verse in John 15 is absolutely incredible and a great place for us to close this section on taking airways and controlling spiritual atmospheres. For thousands of years, humankind had to serve God by either participating in certain systems, adhering to laws, following strict guidelines, etc. While we still serve Him, we have also been given a new identity. Jesus calls us His friends, the same title given to Moses and Abraham. What is unique about this title and these two men? The common ground of intercession.

There are some incredible conversations in the Old Testament between God and His friends—Abraham (see James 2:23) and Moses (see Exod. 33:11)—where their prayers seem to change His mind. And not on small issues either! We are talking about major spiritual shifts taking place over a region or an entire people group.

Can you imagine that? God is absolutely sovereign, but He is also relational. John 15:15 begins to become clearer. Friends are privy to knowing what the Master is doing. Maybe more than changing God's mind, the Master is actually involving His friends and intercessors in the process of executing His will. Whether or not God's mind actually changes, I know this much—the intercessions of God's friends change *outcomes*.

When we read about Abraham's persistent intercession for Sodom and Gomorrah (see Gen. 18:16-33), and later on, Moses' frequent pleas on behalf of Israel (one example: Num. 14:11-20), it is incredible to see that the voice of God's friends carries significant influence before His throne, creating outcomes for entire cities and people groups. You are a friend of God. This means, your voice carries the same weight for cities and people groups.

YOU ARE GOD'S FRIEND.

Doesn't it make sense, though? Beloved friends have the ability to influence us and help us move forward with certain decisions. We might set out to do one thing, but after having lunch with a close friend, our plans could change dramatically. Intercession is the language of friendship between God and humanity. The key for both Abraham and Moses was their knowledge of God's character. This is the standard they reminded Him with when making intercession for entire people groups.

Perhaps He was just waiting for one to arise who would stand in the gap and demonstrate knowledge of who He was—merciful, full of loving-kindness, and true to His promises. Could it be that the Father is waiting for such friends to arise today and raise voices before His throne that could in fact shift destiny over entire nations?

Daily Reflection Questions

1. Why do you think intercession is the "language of God's friends"? Specifically, how does intercession reveal that we are actually embracing our identity as God's friends?

_____

_____

_____

2. How should you as an intercessor understand your identity as God's friend, and how does this empower you to intercede more effectively?

_____

_____

_____

3. In what ways is knowing who God is—*His character and nature*—important when we come before Him in intercession? How did this help Abraham and Moses?

_____

_____

_____

Daily Meditation

The friendship that Moses and Abraham enjoyed with God has been given to all of us through Jesus. This relationship gives us insight into the Father's character and enables us to intercede based on who He is on behalf of entire regions and people groups.

Prayer

> *Father, it is a great joy to be called Your friend. Thank You for giving me access to what Moses and Abraham enjoyed—friendship with You and the knowledge of who You are. Help me to intercede based on Your character. When I see conditions and situations that don't reflect Your nature, embolden me to release Your solutions over those people, cities, nations, or people groups. Thank You that one voice who declares Your heart and says what You are saying is all it takes to supernaturally transform outcomes and bring Your Kingdom to earth!*
> *In Jesus' name,*
> *Amen*

For Additional Study

■ Read *The Happy Intercessor*, pages 114-115.

WAGING WARFARE USING WORSHIP AND JOY

"Two elements in warfare that I feel are our greatest tools of intercession are worship and joy. I believe that these two weapons bring more confusion to the devil's camp than anything else. Both of these weapons of war come out of our intimate relationship with our Father God."

—BENI JOHNSON

Session 6

WAGING WARFARE USING WORSHIP AND JOY

DISCUSSION QUESTIONS

There are _____ ways of interceding.

One of the greatest weapons of warfare is _____.

What Does Your Worship Do?

1. It _____ God.

2. It brings you into the _____ realm.

3. It breaks down _____ because it releases the Kingdom.

4. It _____ the spiritual atmosphere.

5. It changes your _____—off your problem and on-to God.

Joy...

Brings the element of _____.

Releases laughter, which is good _____.

Enables us to _____ in the midst of circumstances.

WARFARE WORSHIP

But thou art holy, O thou that inhabitest the
praises of Israel (Psalm 22:3 KLV).

At first glance, Psalm 22:3 does not look like a warfare Scripture. This is because we need to start approaching worship and warfare differently. When we worship, we have access to the heavenly realm. When this realm is released into the earth—as God inhabits our praise—warfare is taking place. You see, worship warfare involves holding a high view of God and His Presence, while maintaining a low view of the devil.

The truth is, when we worship, we push ourselves out of the inferior first and second realms where we pick up all of the negative stuff, and we enter into the glory realm. This is the realm of God's Presence. This is doing warfare on God's terms, not the devil's. The devil would love us to spend a whole bunch of time focused on him and his tactics, when in fact, that time would be best spent with our eyes on the Father. When our focus is on God, we position ourselves to usher in His power and Presence through intercession. When our focus is on the problem, or on the devil, it becomes difficult to usher in God's power because we become overly aware of the very thing God's power needs to transform. Awareness is everything when it comes to intercession. What we are most aware of tends to fuel how we pray. This is why God-centered worship is so important.

WORSHIP WARFARE HOLDS A HIGH VIEW OF GOD'S PRESENCE AND A LOW VIEW OF THE DEVIL.

In Psalm 68:1, warfare worship is pictured. The psalmist writes, *"Let God arise, let His enemies be scattered."* It is really that simple. When we worship God and His Presence shows up, the result is warfare. God comes and the enemy is scattered. In other words, we are not called to spend all of our energy in intercession fighting and warring and struggling with the devil. The reality is, we have no place fighting against someone who has already been defeated. What an encouragement!

One of the main purposes behind this book and study is to help people see intercession for what it truly is—one of the most joyful things that we, as believers, get to take part in. The key is allowing the Word of God and the Holy Spirit to change our thinking. We need to be open to see things different from what we might have in the past. I am not denying the place for warfare worship at all. In fact, I pray that our eyes are opened to how powerful worship is in releasing Kingdom warfare.

What happens, in my opinion, is that we think *we* are the instruments of warfare in worship. So we push. So we shout. So we exert tremendous energy to dismantle demonic schemes and strategies through worship. I don't know how super spiritual this advice sounds, but I think we really need to chill out a bit. I'm not calling for laziness; I'm calling for a joyful delight in the God we worship and a confident assurance that *He* fights on our behalf as His Presence comes and inhabits our praise.

Daily Reflection Questions

1. What comes to your mind when you think of "warfare worship?"

_____

_____

_____

_____

2. How does focusing our worship on God actually release His Presence to do warfare? (See Psalm 68:10-2.)

_____

_____

_____

3. In what ways have you experienced worship that released warfare? How can these be seen as acts of intercession?

_____

_____

_____

Daily Meditation

Worship releases warfare because worship carries God's Presence. When He inhabits our worship, the enemy must scatter because he must flee from God's Presence.

Prayer

Father, thank You for inhabiting my praise and worship. Thank You for the gift of Your Presence. Help me keep my eyes focused on You in worship and not get distracted by what is going on around me. You are greater than whatever problem or impossibility I am facing. You have already won the victory over the enemy. Help me to simply worship You for who You are, and trust that as You arise and Your Presence is released, the enemy must flee.
In Jesus' name,
Amen

For Additional Study

- Read *The Happy Intercessor*, pages 102-104.

- Read *The Joy of Intercession* devotional, pages 135-138.

Day Two

PRAISE CONFUSES THE ENEMY

*...he [King Jehoshaphat] appointed those who sang to the Lord
and those who praised Him in holy attire, as they went out
before the army and said, "Give thanks to the Lord, for His
lovingkindness is everlasting"* (2 Chronicles 20:21 NASB).

The presence of joy and praise in intercession really confuses the enemy.
It does not make sense, as it is absolutely supernatural. When we are joyful, even as we are praying on behalf of some pretty heavy and weighty
things, I believe our prayers become more effective. Likewise, when we
are able to praise God even when things in those first two realms are
looking pretty negative, our actions actually confuse darkness and wage
warfare upon it.

Joy and praise increase the effectiveness of our intercession. They
make it difficult to just focus on the problem. There is a difference
between praying the problem and releasing the solution.

Now I am not saying that there is no place for experiencing sadness in intercession. Oftentimes, intercession might begin because of an
unexplainable feeling of sadness or even feelings of depression. We are
picking up on stuff going on in the first and second realms. This is normal and actually helps us start to pray. The key is, as we have studied so
far, we cannot pray out of those places. We must pray out of the realm
where victory is the only option and God's reign is absolutely secure.
This is defined by joy and praise.

Intercessors who release solutions through joy and praise will walk in victory.

Let's look at the story of King Jehoshaphat in Second Chronicles 20. I outlined the entire experience in *The Happy Intercessor*, so for right now, I want to focus on one specific part of it. I want us to pay attention to *how* the armies of God waged warfare when dealing with the enemy. Look at their song in verse 21. They were not focusing in on the enemy with their song, but rather giving thanks to the Lord—specifically focusing on His everlasting loving-kindness.

This confuses the enemy because in his warped world it makes sense for people to get caught up in problems and hopelessness. It makes sense to respond to your problem, situation, or circumstance in fear rather than faith. Let me just say, it is absolutely amazing what an understanding of God's goodness will do for you in intercession. As His goodness and loving-kindness is our focus, no matter what is going on around us, we can pray according to who we know God to be. We know He never changes. We know He is good all of the time. When truths like these are our anchors, our attitude in intercession changes, and what we pray begins to release solutions.

Remember this—the intercessor who releases solutions through joy and praise will never cease confusing, and ultimately, walking in victory over the enemy.

Daily Reflection Questions

1.   How do you think praise and joy actually confuse the enemy?

_____

_____

_____

_____

2.   If we tend to only focus on problems in our prayers, what happens?

_____

_____

_____

3.   In what ways is Jehoshaphat's battle song (see 2 Chron. 20:21) sig-
     nificant when it comes to forming your understanding of worship
     and warfare?

_____

_____

_____

Daily Meditation

In intercession, when we maintain an attitude of praise and joy, it
actually confuses the enemy. When we consistently pray the problems,
motivated by fear and hopelessness, we become distracted from focusing
on releasing solutions.

Prayer

*Father, I pray just like King Jehoshaphat did: My eyes are on You.
Thank You Holy Spirit for empowering me to pray answers and
release solutions. I declare that I am not focused on the problems
or the darkness or the opposition. Instead, help me to meditate
upon Your goodness. Your loving-kindness. I thank You that the
enemy is confused and defeated when my attitude is one of joy
and praise because my eyes are on constantly on You!*
In Jesus' name,
Amen

For Additional Study

- Read *The Happy Intercessor*, pages 122-125.
- Read *The Joy of Intercession* devotional, pages 139-142.

JOY AND REST: THE MISSING INGREDIENTS OF INTERCESSION

For My yoke is easy and My burden is light (Matthew 11:30).

This final section of our study represents the heart of why I wrote *The Happy Intercessor* and why we have been on this journey together. At our fingertips is the power of Heaven ready and waiting to be released through our intercession. Why, then, do we not take advantage of the incredible opportunity that is right there waiting for us? I think it is because we see it as something it is not. Jesus' words in Matthew 11 really capture everything that needs to be said when it comes to how we should approach intercession.

Even though we do bring burdens to the Lord in prayer, the "burden" that we are called to carry is not heavy and cumbersome. Jesus said that His yoke is easy, and His burden is light. Since our model is "on earth as it is in Heaven," I would love to go to Heaven for a visit and really get a feel for how joyful and peaceful that culture really is. Even though we have experienced tastes of this, I don't think we can fully comprehend the magnitude of the joy and peace experienced in a world defined by the Father's Presence.

Since Heaven is defined by joy and peace, intercession in Heaven is not one of labor and work. Jesus is our ultimate example of this. As we studied before, when it comes to finding a perfect model for intercession, we need to look no further than Jesus. I am not sure why we have these images of Jesus agonizing as He brings intercession before the throne of God. Agony demonstrates labor, and labor means that work is being done.

JESUS IS THE PERFECT MODEL FOR INTERCESSION.

I love the following verses, as they give us every reason to believe Jesus was a *Happy Intercessor* and this makes it legal for us following in His footsteps: *"And every priest stands ministering daily and offering repeatedly the same sacrifices, which can never take away sins. But this Man, after He had offered one sacrifice for sins forever, sat down at the right hand of God"* (Heb. 10:11-12).

Jesus is compared to the priests under the Old Testament sacrificial system. In that way of doing things, priests "stood" ministering daily, and had to repeatedly offer up sacrifices on behalf of the people. Significant work was involved. Ultimately, these sacrifices could provide temporary atonement, but were unable to permanently "take away sins." Jesus, *this Man*, offered one sacrifice for sin and "sat down." The priests under the Old Covenant of works were always standing, but Jesus, the Author and Finisher of our Faith, "sat down." This means He completed the work and rested. The burden was lifted, and the intercession He ever lives to offer is not frantic and worrisome (see Heb. 7:25).

The work has been done, and the glorious exchange that we get to participate in is coming into agreement with the intercession of Jesus. This happens when we declare His solutions and when we pray what the Father is saying.

Daily Reflection Questions

1. Read Matthew 11:30. Perhaps choose a few different translations to read. Why is it so important for our intercession to be motivated by peace and joy instead of labor and striving?

    ---

2. How do we follow Jesus' example when we remain in a place of peace, rest, and joy in intercession?

    ---

3. What are some specific burdens we need to give over to Jesus when it comes to intercession? How does constantly "carrying" burdens in intercession (not releasing them to Jesus) start making our prayers ineffective?

Daily Meditation

Since the model for ministry is "on earth as it is in Heaven," it is very important for believers to intercede motivated by peace and joy—the very things that define Heaven's culture. By constantly carrying burdens in intercession, we begin to focus more on problems instead of praying the solutions, and we live in a place of unrest.

Prayer

Lord, I'm trading my burden for your peace. My unrest for Your joy. Your yoke is easy, and your burden is light. You told me to cast all of my cares upon You, so Father, that is what I am doing. When I come before Your throne in intercession, I might be motivated to bring a burden before You, but help me to leave it with You. When I turn it over to You, You can release supernatural solutions and answers that I could never accomplish in my own strength.
In Jesus' name,
Amen

For Additional Study:

- Read *The Happy Intercessor*, pages 127-129.

- Read *The Joy of Intercession* devotional, pages 147-150.

JOY: THE FOUNDATION FOR WARFARE

*But now I come to You; and these things I speak
in the world so that they may have My joy made
full in themselves* (John 17:13 NASB).

*J*esus came to give us *His* joy. In fact He *is* our joy. The joy Jesus described in John 17 can only be experienced in Him, and as we keep His Presence our priority. This is why it is so important for us to have a balanced view on "warfare." If we get distracted from joy in Jesus by spending all of our time waging warfare, we start getting intercession backward and are headed down a road toward burnout. I know this entire section has been about waging war through worship and joy. The key is knowing that warfare is released because of our worship and joy—not the other way around.

Our focus should not be on doing the warfare, but instead, the focus should be on Jesus. The results? Worship. When we look at Him, we cannot help but worship Him for who He is. Joy. We cannot help but become outrageously joyful when we consider what He has accomplished. Joy and worship should be our focus, and there should be an expectation that in the background, these things actually produce warfare that tears down strongholds and destroys darkness over people and regions.

JOY AND WORSHIP PRODUCE WARFARE THAT TEARS DOWN STRONGHOLDS AND DESTROYS DARKNESS.

Many people get burned out with intercession because they unnecessarily enter battles they are not fit to win. In *The Happy Intercessor* I share the story of a young Christian who got involved in very works-based intercession. Labor and warfare overwhelmed relationship and intimacy. Back then, we went to church and looked for problems to pray against rather than spending time with our Father, releasing His solutions. The point? The focus was not Jesus, but rather warfare. No wonder we would go home tired and worn out. The unfortunate result for our young friend was burnout. She left the church and didn't want anything to do with intercession (as we had known and practiced it). Why? She told me herself. She was tired of the fighting and working in intercession and felt like she just couldn't do it anymore. Her response changed my life and is one of the factors that led to creating this study.

Again, none of us are fit to do battle with unseen spiritual forces. On the flip side, Jesus has already disarmed these powers and is completely victorious. This is why it is so important to keep Jesus the main emphasis of intercession. This means, you and I must approach warfare from that place. Again, our focus is on the One who is victorious, and we keep everything centered on Him.

When we truly understand what Jesus has accomplished, joy is not optional. In Colossians 2:15 (NASB), we read that God "*had disarmed the rulers and authorities, He made a public display of them, having triumphed over them through Him*" [Jesus].

Daily Reflection Questions

1. Why do you think people can become spiritually burned out on intercession? How does your understanding of warfare determine how you approach intercession?

_____

_____

_____

_____

2. Have you ever experienced spiritual burnout when it comes to intercession, prayer, and/or spiritual warfare? What do you think caused this?

_____

_____

_____

_____

3. How is focusing on Jesus the solution to keeping joy and worship the center of your intercession?

_____

_____

_____

_____

Daily Meditation

In intercession, it is not up to us to do Jesus' job—He already disarmed the powers of darkness. Rather, our stance in intercession should be one of joy, as our sight is fixed on the finished work of Jesus.

Prayer

Father, I am so grateful for the sacrifice of Your Son. Jesus paid it ALL. He paid the full price for every sin, and He destroyed the powers of darkness. Teach me, Holy Spirit, not to strive and do the work that Jesus has already accomplished. Help me to come into agreement with what has been done; and instead of focusing on the warfare, empower me to keep my sights set on Jesus. He is my joy!
In Jesus' name,
Amen

For Additional Study

- Read *The Happy Intercessor*, pages 130-131.

SURPRISED BY JOY

"Surprise is a viable principle of war." —*Robert R. Leonhard*

I thought that this would be an ideal place for us to end our journey together. I pray that the Holy Spirit has been doing a work in your heart, showing you what a blessing and benefit intercession is for the Christian life. The key is seeing the necessary place of joy in the life of the intercessor.

To be a *happy intercessor* is the fruit of one whose gaze is fixed on Jesus instead of the problems or warfare, and one who has surrendered his or her burdens over to Him completely. It is not a badge of honor for intercessors to lug around every single burden on the planet. This image of intercession must change. Thankfully, we are witnessing a significant shift in this area.

This I know. When joyful intercessors rise across the nations and begin to release God's solutions through their declarations—even in the midst of horrendous problems and impossible circumstances—power will be released that takes the devil completely by surprise. I talk about this in *The Happy Intercessor,* specifically explaining the element of surprise and how it relates to joyful intercession. In wartime, this principle of surprise is very important in experiencing victory over the enemy. The same is true for you and me.

THE ENEMY IS UNREADY FOR A PEOPLE WHO INTERCEDE OUT OF A PLACE OF JOY.

In *The Armchair General* magazine, Robert R. Leonhard writes: "Surprise, then, is a principle of war that is alive and well. It is an enduring feature of warfare, because its components—time and perpetual unreadiness—are immutable." The enemy is unready for a people who intercede out of a place of joy. This stance in prayer consistently produces results.

When I say "produces results," I am not implying that God does not hear intercession that is burden-focused. In His grace and mercy, I know He is attentive to the cries of His people. That said, I want this resource that we have been going through together to help disciple you to live in a place of consistent victory. For the believer, life should not be a series of ups, downs, highs and lows. This is not to say trouble does not come. It does. The key is responding in a manner that surprises the enemy and enforces the victory secured at Calvary.

We end where we began: *On earth as it is in Heaven*. My prayer for you is that as your heart is rooted in His world (Heaven) and His realm, your intercession will change the world around you. You no longer pray from a place of striving or labor; but instead, your prayers are in agreement with the Father's heart. Your words reflect and release the words of Jesus. And finally, your intercession joyfully brings God's world and Kingdom to this one.

Daily Meditation

When intercessors pray out of the place of joy, this takes darkness by surprise. The enemy expects people to respond to problems with fear and anxiety; he is not expecting people who respond to problems by releasing solutions through intercession.

For Additional Study

- Read *The Happy Intercessor*, pages 131-132.

Prayer

Instead of answering the Daily Reflection Questions today, I invite you to spend a little longer in the place of prayer. We study not to get more information, but to become better equipped for activation. My heart for this curriculum is to help activate you to not only know what it means to be a *happy intercessor,* but show you how to become one and bring God's solutions to situations that need His supernatural intervention.

ANSWER KEY

Session 1

Intimacy
Heartbreak, love
Agenda
Sensitive
Ideas

Session 2

Offense
Fear
Good
Focused, mark
Word
Principalities
Little

Session 3

Joy
Worry, fear
Perspective
Authority

Session 4

Visible, physical
Angelic, demonic

Glory
Pray
Third
Presence
Inform

Session 5

Atmosphere
Shift
Memory
Presence
Intersects

Session 6

Different
Joy
Kisses
Heavenly
Resistance
Shifts
Focus
Surprise
Medicine
Laugh

LOOKING FOR MORE
FROM BENI JOHNSON
AND BETHEL CHURCH?

Purchase additional resources—CDs, DVDs, digital downloads, music—from Beni Johnson and the Bethel team at the online Bethel store. Visit www.benij.org for more information on Beni Johnson, to view her speaking itinerary, or to search for additional teaching resources. To order Bethel Church resources, visit http://store.ibethel.org.

Subscribe to iBethel.TV to access the latest sermons, worship sets, and conferences from Bethel Church. To subscribe, visit www.ibethel.tv.

Become part of a supernatural culture that is transforming the world and *apply* for the Bethel School of Supernatural Ministry. For more information, visit www.ibethel.org/school-of-ministry.

LOOKING FOR MORE GREAT CURRICULUM?

Visit HostingThePresence.com to learn more.

SOW THIS BOOK INTO SOMEONE'S LIFE

Don't let the impact of this book end with you!
Call us today and get a discount when you order 3 or more books to sow into someone else's life.

1-800-987-7033

GET A FREE E-BOOK EVERY MONTH!

www.DestinyImage.com

Visit our site today and sign up for our Weekly Newsletter and you'll get a **Free E-Book Every Month** as our way of thanking you for your support.

Exclusive interviews with your favorite authors only at:

TheVoiceOfDestiny.org

Tune in today!

facebook.com/DestinyImage • twitter.com/DestinyImage